Read.

Pray.

GROW.

365 DAILY DEVOTIONAL

Donna,

Thank you for the support.

Blessings,

LaDonna

LaDonna Michele

Printed in the United States of America

Book Cover Design: Studio 5 Agency (www.studio5agency.com)

ISBN 978-1978417939
Keen Vision Publishing, LLC
www.keen-vision.com

"If you abide in Me, and My words abide in you, ask whatever you wish, and it will be done for you."

John 15:7

Contents

Introduction

Growing in the character of Christ is the most important thing in the life of a Christian. From the moment we become "baby believers" and accept Christ into our lives, we begin to grow and mature in our relationship with Christ. We continue to grow and develop throughout our Christian journey until we become "seasoned saints."

Spiritual growth is similar to physical growth. With proper nutrition, exercise, and rest, our bodies (both physical and spiritual) grow and develop. If we fail to provide our physical and spiritual bodies with essential nutrients, exercise, and rest, our growth and development will be delayed.

Spiritual growth requires proper nutrition from the Word of God. Hebrews 4:12 (NIV) tells us the benefits of studying, "For the word of God is living and active. Sharper than any double-edged sword, penetrates even to dividing soul and spirit, joints and marrow; it judges the thoughts and attitudes of the heart." The more we study, the more scripture remains in our hearts. Studying scripture helps us with life challenges and our struggles with sin. Proverbs 4:10-13 (NIV) says, "Listen, my son, accept what I say, and the years of your life will be many. I instruct you in the way of wisdom and have lead you along straight paths. When you walk, your step will not be hampered; when you run, you will not stumble. Hold on to instruction, and do not let it go; guard it well, for it is your life!" 2 Timothy 3:16-17(NKJV) tells us that studying helps up to serve God better, "All scripture is given by inspiration of God, and is profitable for doctrine, for reproof, for correction, for instruction in righteousness, that the man of God may be complete, thoroughly equipped for every good work. We can also refer to 2 Timothy 2:15 (NKJV) which says, "Be diligent to present yourself approved to God, a worker who does not need to be ashamed, rightly dividing the word of truth." Just as our bodies need physical food, they need spiritual food.

Reading and studying God's Word allows us to get to know Jesus. It equips us to be a disciple (follower) of Christ. It brings joy into our lives. It makes us more knowledgeable of the things of God. A 2013 Huffington Post article found science-based benefits to reading including: relaxation, keeping our brains sharp, helping us sleep better, and increasing empathy. If reading ordinary books can do all that, imagine what reading the Word of God can do!

Another essential to spiritual growth is to exercise prayer daily. Prayer reminds us that God hears His children. Psalm 66:18 reminds us how our sin hinders our prayer. We should pray to defeat our enemy, Satan. We should pray because it places us in direct communication with God and puts God in direct communication with us. We should pray because the prayers of a right-living person are powerful and effective. James 5:16 (NKJV) says, "The prayer of a righteous man is powerful and effective." According to a 2013 Pew Research Poll, over half of Americans pray every day. A 2012 poll found that over 75 percent of Americans believe that prayer is an important part of daily life. Other polls indicate that some atheists and religiously unaffiliated individuals admit that they pray. Scientific research suggests that prayer may be very beneficial. This research shows that prayer improves self-control, increases kindness, allows us to be more forgiving, increases our ability to trust, and off-sets the negative impacts of stress. These results are very synonymous with what happens as we grow in the character of Christ.

Finally, healthy spiritual and physical growth requires sufficient rest. A 2012 Healthy Living article cited ten physical health benefits of relaxation. According to this article, sufficient rest allows us to protect our hearts, lowers our risk of catching a cold, boots memory, lowers our risk of stroke, and helps us make better decisions. It is my hope that because you are reading this devotional, you are seeking to grow in the character of Christ. These devotionals can help you do just that—READ. PRAY. GROW. Repeat.

READ—Read Examine Accept Delight (2 Timothy 3:16-17)
PRAY—Praise Repent Ask Yield (1 Thessalonians 5:17)
GROW—Greet Review Observe Walk (James 4:7)

JANUARY

January 1
STONES OF REMEMBRANCE

"Then you shall answer them that the waters of the Jordan were cut off before the ark of the covenant of the Lord; when it crossed over the Jordan, the waters of the Jordan were cut off. And these stones shall be for a memorial to the children of Israel forever."
Joshua 4:7 (NKJV)

What will we tell our children, nieces, nephews, and younger cousins about the goodness of the Lord? We can be certain that difficult times will fall upon each of our lives at some point. In addition to prayer, we can withstand these times by remembering God's faithfulness in past seasons of our lives. We should mark the significant moments in our lives, the doors God has opened, and the difference He has made in our lives. We should be able to share these testimonies with those closest to us to encourage them on their walk as well.

What memorial stones have you established in your life? Is there a song you frequently sing? A scripture you often repeat and stand on daily? We should have some memorial stones or stones of remembrance. We should mark those moments in such a way that people notice their significance and ask us to share their importance in our lives. What are your stones of remembrance? What songs do you sing? What scriptures do you hold near and dear? Let those be your memorial stones. Don't be afraid to share them with those who may be in need of a reminder that they are victorious in Christ!

Lord, let me continually place stones of remembrance in my walk with you so that I never forget the things you have done in my life.

January 2
SOUL SISTERS/BROTHERS

"the soul of Jonathan was knit to the soul of David, and Jonathan loved him as his own soul."

1 Samuel 18:1b

There are different levels of relationships. We have acquaintances, friends, and also those who are like family whom we refer to as *sis* or *bro*. Each category being more selective than the previous categories. Acquaintances know the good, friends know the good and the bad, and sis/bro knows the good, bad, and the ugly. Sis/Bro is there in tears of joy and tears of sorrow. Sis/Bro tells you the truth in love and helps you walk in that truth. This level of relationship is special and is such a blessing. It is possible because the people in the relationship love God. Their loving relationship with the Lord is mirrored in their relationship with one another. Their souls have been tied together. This is the relationship Johnathan and David shared. The Bible tells us that their souls were knitted together and that they loved one another as they loved themselves. We get two wonderful examples which are the soul ties between Godly friends and the soul ties we have with God, our father. We are blessed to have both in our lives. At the same time, we should guard both relationships from those who would seek to sever our soul ties. We must also be careful who we tie our souls to here on Earth. We should choose godly friends who love us with unconditional love, just as our heavenly father-friend does.

Lord, give me godly friends that continue to tie my soul to you. Help me to discern the soul ties I have in my life. Give me the strength to sever the ties that do not draw me closer to you.

LaDonna Michele

January 3
UNDIGNIFIED PRAISE

*"David replied to Michal, "In God's presence I'll dance all I want!
...Oh yes, I'll dance to God's glory—more recklessly even than
this. And as far as I'm concerned . .I'll gladly look like a fool."*

2 Samuel 6:21 (MSG)

Music is one of the most powerful forces on Earth. It can move the hardest of hearts to tears. Whether instrumental or with lyrics, music is a powerful force. The combination of instrumentals and lyrics take us on wonderful journeys of sight, sound, and feeling. This is especially true with gospel music. The message in the music saturates our souls and penetrates our hearts. I imagine that this is the indescribable joy David felt upon the return of the ark. His soul was overwhelmed by the worship music. It moved his heart and spirit and caused his very body to dance! That act was totally out of character for a king. In those times, a king was expected to conduct himself with the utmost decorum at all times. But when David saw the ark returning and reflected on the goodness of God in his own life—he broke out in dance. The most impressive point was even when his wife told him to be more dignified, his reply was to give God more praise. The more he thought about the goodness of God, the more *undignified* he became! The truth in gospel music should be what moves men, not the downbeat or the talented lyricist. We should be moved by the truth of the words and the difference that truth has made in our lives. When we think of the goodness of God in our lives, we should give praise and worship to God without concern for what others think. Consider King David who danced right out of his clothes! Undignified praise. God deserves it.

Lord, let my praise be based only on what you think.

8

January 4
WHAT YOU WANT

"In those days there was no king in Israel; everyone did whatever he wanted."

Judges 21:25 (HCSB)

What happens when a teacher steps out of the classroom for one minute? Chaos! From kindergarten to college, when the teacher or professor leaves, each student takes it upon themselves to do whatever they want to do. The same is true in our flesh. When we fail to put our flesh in check with our spirit purposely, the flesh takes over and does whatever it wants.

The flesh wants what it wants, when it wants it, and how it wants it. It fails to remind us that there are serious consequences to doing whatever we want. Like the children of Israel in the scripture above, we sometimes get so caught up in doing whatever we want to do that we don't realize the consequences until it is too late. In the process, we pass up perfect for good. This is exactly what happened in the text. God's original plan for man was to be his King, and no earthly king would be needed for the children of God. As a result, they rebelled, doing whatever they wanted. Eventually, the children of Israel wanted to be like other nations who had earthly kings. They were so determined to do whatever they wanted that they missed the blessing. They missed the Great King before them and desired a good earthly king. The danger in doing what we want is that we don't know what we are doing. We are safest when we instead do whatever God wants.

Lord, do not allow me to get so caught up in doing what I want to do that I miss the blessing of doing what you want me to do.

January 5
THANK YOU FOR BEING A FRIEND

"In the same way that iron sharpens iron, a person sharpens the character of his friend."

Proverbs 27:17 (VOICE)

The 1980's TV show, *The Golden Girls*, is a TV classic. The show followed the lives of three best friends living together in their *golden years* in Miami, Florida. The best thing about the show was the opening song:

> *Thank you for being a friend, traveled down the road and back again, your heart is true you're a pal and a confidant. And if you through a party, invited everyone you knew. You would see the biggest gift would be from me and the card attached would say, 'thank you for being a friend.*

The lyrics of the song provide a profound definition of both earthly and heavenly friendships. We desire friends who will travel through the ups and downs of life with us. We desire friends with pure hearts. We desire friends who will be our confidant. Most of all, we desire friends who will sharpen our character. We have been given such a friend in Christ.

Christ, today, we thank you for being a friend. You have traveled down the road of life with us and knew the end from the beginning. Your heart is true, and you are not only our confidant, but you are also our comforter and Savior. You sharpen our character into your character. Jesus, thank you for being a friend.

Lord, thank you for friends that have you as a friend. Help me to sharpen my friends just as you sharpen me.

January 6
NO SHAME IN MY GAME

"For I am not ashamed of the gospel, because it is God's power for salvation to everyone who believes."

Romans 1:16 (HCSB)

A re you a Christian?" I was asked this question while waiting in line at the snack bar at work. Without hesitation or second thought I replied, "Yes." The answer to that question is now automatic, but it wasn't always that way. Depending on the situation or persons in my vicinity, the answer to that question varied and fluctuated. Sometimes I responded with confidence, other times not so much. It wasn't until I understood and appreciated the gift of salvation that I was able to proudly proclaim that I am a Christian. There is no shame in what Christ has done for us. The gospel is the power for salvation if we only believe. We are empowered through salvation to be a witness to the truth of the gospel. Once that penetrates our souls, we can't help but to be unashamed. Confessing to being a Christian should bring us great joy. We should strive to live our lives in such a way that we will not be ashamed of the gospel.

Lord, let me tell others that I am a Christian with both my lips and my life, for I am not ashamed of the Gospel. I know personally that it is the power unto salvation.

January 7

T.H.I.N.K. BEFORE YOU REPEAT

"And when the children of Israel heard of it, the whole congregation of the children of Israel gathered together at Shiloh to go to war against them."

Joshua 22:11-2, 31-34

Have you ever played the telephone game? One person whispers a message in the ear of the person next to them, then that person passes the message on, and this repeats until the last person is reached and attempts to repeat the original statement. Almost inevitably, the final statement is never the original statement. Somewhere along the way, the message gets twisted and changed. The misunderstood parts are filled in with another person's interpretation. The more the message is passed along, the more distorted it becomes. A similar thing occurs with adults. Whether it's texting or posting on Facebook, we take bits and pieces of what we think we heard without clarification, verification, or many times correct information. We embellish and expand for added effect as well. The result can be damaging. Before we react, repeat, or repost we must condition ourselves to T.H.I.N.K. Is it True, Helpful, Inspiring, Necessary, Kind? You know you are growing in God when you hear a rumor, and it stops with you, you don't repeat it, and you have no desire to do so.

Lord, let me guard my ears, what they hear and guard my tongue, what it says. Let me always T.H.I.N.K. before I speak.

January 8
PERSISTENT IN PRAYER

"And she was in bitterness of soul, and prayed to the Lord and wept in anguish."

1 Samuel 1:10 (HCSB)

As children, we recite prayers to get us in the practice of praying. We say, *God Is Great, God is Good* before each meal and, *Now I Lay Me Down to Sleep*, before bed. When we get a little older, we progress to The Lord's Prayer. Life will take your prayers further if you allow it. The emphasis will then be on talking to God openly, honestly, and persistently. This is how our prayer lives should grow. Life will move us to persistent prayer just as it did Hannah. Life forced Hannah to pour her heart out to the Lord daily in prayer. No one but God understood her pain and anguish over being barren. Hannah persistently approached God in prayer so that He would open her womb. Not only did she pray out loud with her voice, but she also prayed in her heart, and prayed in her tears. She did so sincerely, without reservation. Her prayers were persistent. Her persistence moved the heart of God.

Lord, let me persist in prayer to you throughout the day. Whether audible or silent, thank you.

13

January 9
IT BEGINS WITH LOYALTY

"When she saw that she was determined to go with her, she stopped speaking to her. "

Ruth 1:18

My dad is retired from the Army (yes, I am a military brat). The Army has an acronym for their values: LDRSHIP—Loyalty, Duty, Respect, Selfless Service, Honor, Integrity, and Personal courage. I have watched my father embody these values all my life. Another person who comes to mind when I consider these seven core values is Ruth. While she undoubtedly possesses all of them, the one that stands out the most is loyalty. If we follow the Army values model, it all begins with loyalty. Ruth was the daughter-in-law of Naomi. Naomi lost her husband and her two sons, one of which was the husband of Ruth. Unlike what we would expect, Ruth refused to return to where she came from and instead remained loyal to Naomi. She even went so far as to tell Naomi, "Where you go, I will go and your God will be my God." She stayed committed to Naomi even when she had become bitter because of the loss of her husband and sons. Loyalty allows us to love those we care about most, even when they are not so lovable. Our loyalty gives us the strength love them through their hurts and pains.

Lord, let me be loyal first to you, but also to those you have placed in my life.

January 10
TAKE IT TO THE KING

"Go home in peace. I have heard what you said and have granted your request."

1 Samuel 25:35

A meme appeared on my Facebook timeline that said, "Have you prayed about it as much as you have talked about it?" Often, we run and tell our problems to a spouse or close friend. We give our perspective, then sit and wait patiently for their response. So often, God is not our first contact, but rather our last resort. Our situations would turn out a lot different if we would take our issues to him first. In the text above, Abigail took it upon herself to go directly to King David regarding her husband. Now, her husband was an evil and cruel man and everyone knew it. Rather than bad mouthing her husband or seeking advice from friends, she went directly to the king. We should do the same.

When life places us in difficult situations, our first response should be to go to the Lord in prayer. Whatever it is, we should first take it to the King.

Lord, let my first response always be to take my problems to you.

January 11

PERPETUAL PRAISE

"I will bless the Lord at all times; His praise shall continually be in my mouth."

Psalm 34:1

One of my favorite Michael Jackson songs is "Don't Stop Until You Get Enough." The music, vocals, and the hook all work together to make you want to keep dancing. I feel the same way about the Justin Timberlake song "Can't Stop the Feeling." Both songs make you want to dance, dance, dance. We should get the same excitement when we enter the house of the Lord. We should come to every worship experience with great expectation about what the Lord will do. Praise doesn't just begin when we enter the sanctuary; it is perpetual.

As the psalmist says, we should bless the Lord all the time. Praises unto God should continually be in our mouths.

Lord, let me always have my heart positioned to praise.

January 12
NEW DAY, NEW MERCIES, SAME GOD

"Through the Lord's mercies we are not consumed, because His compassions fail not. They are new every morning; Great is Your faithfulness."

Lamentations 3:22-23

I love to read! It is one of my greatest joys. Fellow bookworms can understand the excitement I have when I take on a new book. It is the anticipation of what lies inside. Each morning should be a similar experience in our daily lives. Each morning, we awake to a new day full of new mercy, but the same God! We should be excited with the anticipation of what God has in store for us that day. Instead of running to complete your to-do list, try using the first five minutes after you wake up to thank God. Start your day with gratitude and appreciation. When you start your day off with gratitude, you will be better prepared for everything that comes your way! Challenge yourself to begin your days in God's presence.

Lord, thank you for the new day and new mercy you provide every day. I want you to be the first thing on my mind when I wake up and the last thing I think about before I go to sleep.

January 13
LOOK LIKE DADDY

"So God created man in His own image; in the image of God He created him; male and female He created them."

Genesis 1:27

I am a daddy's girl. I can admit that without shame. My father and I have very similar personalities, senses of humor, and physical characteristics. Since I was a little girl, people always commented on how much I resemble my daddy. I take this as a compliment because of the character of my dad. How much more should we be proud to reflect the image of our heavenly father? The scripture above reminds us that God made us in His image. We should reflect the character of Christ to the point that people will say we look like our heavenly Father. We should want to look like our Daddy.

Lord, thank you for creating me in your image. Forgive me when I am a poor example of who you are. Help me to reflect your character daily and in doing so remind others of who my Father is.

January 14
GIVE GOD YOUR BEST

"And in the process of time it came to pass that Cain brought an offering of the fruit of the ground to the Lord. Abel also brought of the firstborn of his flock and of their fat. And the Lord respected Abel and his offering."

Genesis 4:3-4

My husband and I work together to install the spirit of excellence in our children. We want them to take pride in everything they do, from cleaning their rooms to doing their homework. As I am sure you know, this often requires telling them that some tasks they rush through are unacceptable. This is especially true when it comes to homework. If it is not their best, it is not accepted and must be done over again. In the text, Cain did not give God his best. We do not have all the details, but we can note that Able *brought the firstborn of his flock* while Cain *brought an offering of the fruit of the ground.* The text does not state that Cain brought the first fruits of the harvest. How many times have we given God our sloppy seconds? Whatever we do or give unto the Lord should be done with a spirit of excellence. Anything less than our best is unacceptable.

Lord, thank you for giving me your best in your son Jesus. Forgive me when I do not give you my best. Help me to daily give you the best of everything I have including my time, talent, and treasure.

January 15
EYES STRAIGHT AHEAD

"Do not look behind you nor stay anywhere in the plain."
Genesis 19:17

Since having children, I have developed a bad habit of looking back at them while driving. We can develop the same bad habit in our daily lives, looking backward instead of forward. Staying stuck in what was or could have been rather than what is. This is dangerous. God designed our lives to face and move forward. Think about it. We are anatomically made to face and move forward. Our eyes face forward so we can see where we are going. Our feet face forward to move us forward. It is, therefore, dangerous for us to look back. There can be serious consequences for doing so as we see in the scripture.

Lot and his family were instructed to move forward quickly and not to look back. While Lot and his children did just that, his wife did not. She suffered the consequences of refusing to move forward. The same is true in our daily lives. Failure to move forward and stop looking back can have serious consequences for us spiritually, emotionally, and even physically. Following the guidance of God's word, we can move forward in confidence and obedience.

Lord, thank you for your guidance in my daily life. Forgive me when I fail to obey your word.

January 16
Here I Am To Worship

"And behold, a woman in the city who was a sinner, when she knew that Jesus sat at the table in the Pharisee's house, brought an alabaster flask of fragrant oil."

Luke 7:36-50

I love Cee Cee Winans' description of the scene in her song "Alabaster Box." When I go before God in my private prayer closet or public corporate worship, I go to pour out my praise. I'm not concerned with how others may view my worship. I know that they were not there to witness how God has blessed me. They can't understand how He pulled me through some very difficult circumstances. In the scripture above, the woman brought the alabaster box and poured the expensive oil on Jesus' feet. The disciples looked upon this, and felt that the woman had wasted the expensive oil. In other words, they thought she was *doing too much.* In certain settings and situations, you will encounter people who may think your worship, adoration, and praise may be a little bit *too much.* Never mind them. They don't know what God has done for you, so there is no way they can understand your praise. As long as your praise is sincere and from the heart, give God everything you've got! He's been just that good!

Lord, let me not be ashamed to bring you my best worship and praise regardless of what others around me may think or believe!

January 17

RUNNING, ENDURING, WINNING

"Therefore we also, since we are surrounded by so great a cloud of witnesses, let us lay aside every weight, and the sin which so easily ensnares us, and let us run with endurance the race that is set before us."

Hebrews 12:1

I was a sprinter on my high school track team. I thoroughly enjoyed running the 100m, 200m, and 400m sprints. My coach tried me once on the 800m, and that is not a sprint! It is an endurance race. The Christian life is a race. It's not a sprint like I ran in high school, it's a distance race. It is a race to test and build our endurance. It is not given to the swift or the strong, but to those who endure until the end. That tells us that the race is not going to be easy, and distance races never are. It does tell us that the key is to press. Sometimes, we will be running for Jesus. Sometimes, we will be walking with Jesus. Sometimes, we will be bent over by battles, catching our breath, and struggling to keep our focus on Jesus, but that is the key; to press toward the mark. Keep making forward progress even if all you can do is keep looking forward. Fact is, no matter what happened in the past (loss, financial hardship, unemployment, marriage problems, sickness, wayward children, impurity, sin), we are still victorious through Christ Jesus! We already won! You are still standing; you are still in the race! So, let us run this race with ENDURANCE!

Lord, when my way gets weary, help me to endure to the end.

January 18
...BUT GOD...

"But as for you, ye thought evil against me; but God meant it unto good, ... to save much people alive"

Genesis 50:20

One of my favorite phrases in the Bible is, "but God." These two little words proclaim an intentional intervention. They signal a change, contrast, or clarification is coming next. "But God." What follows this significant transition is intended to challenge our faith and change our life. When He is brought into the picture, God makes all the difference. Take some time to look up the "But God" verses in the Bible.

Joseph had a rough life. He was hated and mocked by his brothers. Sold into slavery and thrown in jail...but God! He may have begun in the pit, but he ended his life in a palace. Not only that, his preservation was to bless others as well! No matter what we face in our lives, we can have confidence knowing that God will intentionally intervene.

Lord, thank you that every "but God" in our lives has been an intentional intervention on our behalf. What is a situation in your life when all you can say on this side of it is "but God"?

January 19

LET THE DEAD STAY DEAD

"I have come that they may have life, and that they may have it more abundantly."

John 10:10

Death is all around us. I'm not just speaking of physical death. I have seen the death of relationships, commitments, and even the death of relationships with the Lord. Where we would find it grotesque for someone to be living with a corpse, we are not so easily offended when people walk around with, associate with, and live with other dead things in their lives. We know the relationship, friendship, or situation is dead, but we continue to drag it around! Why? We do it because it's familiar, comfortable, and we are afraid to trust God. Jesus came that we may have LIFE and have it more abundantly! It's time to rid ourselves of dead connections, relationships, and even friendships. We must trust that God will replace those connections with the people we need to help us move forward in our walk!

Jesus, I know that you came that I may have life and have it more abundantly. Let me abundantly live my life. Give me the strength to rid my life of dead friendships and connections!

January 20
PRAISE GOD FOR SAYING NO

"Father, if you are willing, take this cup from me; yet not my will, but yours be done."

Luke 22:42

Since childhood, we have come to understand "no" as a negative response. We associate it with rejection or keeping us from something we desire. I have learned that instead of complaining about not getting what I asked God for, I should be praising God that He did not give me what I requested. Look back over the past pages of your life, especially your late teens and twenties. Could we praise God on just surviving those ridiculous and immature prayers? A "no" from God is the best answer. God sees the beginning from the ending, and He knows what is best for us. God even told his only son "no" while he prayed earnestly in the garden. If God tells Jesus "no," then we can be sure that the same answer will come in our own lives. We should trust God because He knows what is best for us, even if that answer is "no."

Lord, thank you for saying no even when I desired a yes. Help me to praise you when your answer is no.

January 21
PRAYER IS A PRIVILEGE

"This is the confidence we have in approaching God: that if we ask anything according to his will, he hears us."

1 John 5:14

As children of God, we have been granted the listening ear of a loving God. The Bible tells us we can be confident in approaching God in prayer. We must be humble in our approach, giving reverence to who God is. When we do that and ask according to His will and not our own, He hears us. Not only that, our God loves His own so much that He is sending the answer before we finish speaking! Meditate on that. Not only does God know what we will ask before we ask, but he we also send the answer before we finish speaking! What a privilege prayer is. Who wouldn't want to talk to a God like that?

Lord, thank you for allowing me to bring all my concerns to you in prayer. Draw me even closer to you in prayer. Let me be in constant communication with you regarding all areas of my life.

January 22
DON'T LOOK BACK

"As soon as they had brought them out, one of them said, "Flee for your lives! Don't look back, and don't stop anywhere in the plain! Flee to the mountains or you will be swept away!"

Genesis 19:17

Everyone has a past. We have things we don't want others to know anything about and the things we are ashamed of having done or said. Sometimes, our past haunts us. The past tries to change our focus. That is a trick of the enemy. He uses our past to remind us who we were and what we constantly did. God designed our bodies to make us face forward. It is physically difficult to turn around or look backward. It is virtually impossible to look backward while moving forward. The same goes for our spirits. Trying to look back while moving forward is dangerous and can have some very adverse outcomes. Lot's wife did just that. She attempted to go forward while looking backward. Even after she was warned not to do so, she continued to try to look back. As a result, she ended up turning into a pillar of salt. It is God's design that we keep our focus forward. When our focus is on what is ahead instead of what lies behind we can make more assured footsteps toward the future.

Lord, thank you for the lessons of my past. Let me walk forward focused on what lies ahead and not what lies behind.

January 23
I HEAR YOU

"...And while they are still speaking, I will hear."

Isaiah 65:24

My husband is my best friend. He knows the good, bad, and the ugly of my life. He knows my likes and dislikes. He knows me better than anyone else. Our relationship is so intimate that he can finish my sentences. That hasn't always been true. We had to develop a rapport with one another. This only came from spending time talking and listening to one another. But even my husband does not know me as well as God does. As children of God, we have been granted the listening ear of a living God. Not only that, God loves His own so much that He is sending the answer before we finish speaking! God not only knows what we will ask before we even ask; He also sends the answer before we finish talking. To know God on this level, we must allow ourselves to develop an intimate relationship with Him through prayer and worship.

Lord, thank you for knowing me personally and intimately. I don't even need to finish speaking because you already know the concerns of my heart.

January 24
POSITIONED TO PRAY

"But when you pray, go into your room, close the door and pray to your Father, who is unseen. Then your Father, who sees what is done in secret, will reward you."

Matthew 6:6

I used to find it difficult to pray. Prayer, to me, was very ritualistic and structured, so that is how my prayers came out. It was when I truly understood that prayer is based on the position of my heart, more so than the position of my body, that my prayer life changed.

Prayer is defined as communication with God. To communicate with God, we must be in a relationship with him. Only when we are in a relationship with God can we position ourselves to communicate with him in prayer. The proper position to pray has nothing to do with the physical position of your body, but the spiritual position of your heart. While certain prayer positions are biblical and reveal a level of reverence, they are not mandatory for us to pray to God. Let us be more concerned with the posture of our hearts rather than our bodies.

Lord, position my heart to pray to you.

January 25

FALSE EVIDENCE APPEARING REAL (FEAR)

"For God hath not given us the spirit of fear; but of power, and of love, and of a sound mind."

2 Timothy 1:7

What are you afraid of? Isn't it funny how our fears change over the years? As a child, I was afraid of global warming. As a teen, I was afraid of not getting a scholarship to college. In college, I was afraid of failing. As a young adult, I feared never getting married. A lot of what we are afraid of is based on assumptions. Realistically, it is based on the enemy making evidence appear real. However, the Word of God tells us that fear is not of God. God has not given us a spirit of fear, but of love, power, and a sound mind. Thanks be to God that when fear creeps in, we can stand on faith and know that God has given us power, love, and a sound mind.

Lord, thank you for giving us your power, your love, and a sound mind.

January 26
WE SHEEP

"The Lord is my shepherd, I lack nothing."

Psalm 23: (NIV)

Sheep are not the brightest of God's creations. To be honest, neither are humans. In fact, we have quite a bit in common with sheep. According to Charles Swindoll, in his book, *Living the Psalms*, some characteristics of sheep include:

- Defenseless
- Easily Frightened
- Unclean
- Dependent on Shepherd

As believers, we cannot guide ourselves. We need our Shepherd. We need the protection of the Shepherd. We only find comfort with the Shepherd. We need the Shepherd to clean us up. We need the Shepherd to supply our needs. We find comfort in knowing that we have a "good Shepherd." He guides us beside quiet waters and along the right paths. He is with us in dangerous valleys and comforts us. He anoints us and ensures that we lack nothing. We sheep are in good hands with the good Shepherd.

Lord, I am a sheep and you are my shepherd. Let me follow you in the right paths.

January 27

I'M SORRY

"For I acknowledge my transgressions, And my sin is always before me."

Psalm 51:3

There are different levels of *sorry*. I like to think of it as the *sorry not sorry* phenomenon. "I'm sorry," has become a phrase used time and time again without sincerity but merely to appease. The sincerity of the phrase can be acknowledged just by the way the person says it. We can be so nonchalant with this phrase that it has come to have almost no meaning or merit. Not so with David in Psalm 51. There is nothing flippant or insincere in David. In the scripture above, he pours out his heart out to the Lord for the sin he has committed. It is said that this Psalm was written following the incident with Bathsheba and her husband. (See 2 Samuel 11-12) Having been called out for his sinful deeds by the prophet Samuel, David repents to the Lord.

The key to this Psalm is the acknowledgment of the sin. David doesn't hide his wrongdoing but instead places it on full display so he may be cleansed and forgiven of his sin. What a great lesson this is. God deserves more than "I'm sorry" from us when we sin. We should acknowledge our transgression, confess, and turn from it.

Lord, I acknowledge my transgressions. I confess that I am a sinner and I need your forgiveness.

January 28
AGE AIN'T NOTHING BUT A NUMBER

"…It is now forty-five years since God spoke this word to Moses, years in which Israel wandered in the wilderness. And here I am today, eighty-five years old! I'm as strong as I was the day Moses sent me out. "

Joshua 14:11 (MSG)

For Mother's Day recently, my husband and children bought me a bicycle so that we could ride together as a family. I surprised myself at my ability to still ride a bike and even do a few tricks. My children were impressed as well. The saying is true; you never forget how to ride a bicycle. Thirty years later, I can ride a bike as well as when I was eight years old. The same should be true for our Christian walk. In our key verse, Joshua is declaring the faithfulness of the Lord. At first glance, it appears that he is bragging about himself. However, he is speaking to the keeping power of the Lord. Just as I can ride a bike at thirty-eight just like I could at age eight, God enabled Joshua to do at eighty-five what he did at forty-five. God sustains us in our Christian walk, no matter how old we are. He uses eight-year-olds, forty-five-year-olds, and eighty-five-year-olds, if they are willing to be used.

Lord, use me at every stage of my life. Do not allow me to use age as an excuse.

January 29
AS FOR ME AND MY HOUSE

"And if it seems evil to you to serve the Lord, choose for yourselves this day whom you will serve, whether the gods which your fathers served that were on the other side of the River, or the gods of the Amorites, in whose land you dwell. But as for me and my house, we will serve the Lord."

Joshua 24:15

One of my favorite movies of all times is, *A Raisin in the Sun.* I love the entire movie, but one of the most powerful scenes is where Mrs. Younger (Mama) tells her daughter, Benetha, to repeat after her: "In my mother's house, there is still God." It is a powerful scene and it reflects upon the words of Joshua. Growing up, church was never an option for me. I attended Sunday morning worship, Sunday School, and Bible Study weekly. The only exceptions were sickness. But if you were sick Sunday morning, you were sick all day Sunday. My husband and I have made the same bold stand in our house. Our house serves the Lord. Even though both of my children are young, they understand that we worship on Sunday and attend Sunday School. We also attend Bible Class on Wednesday. As for me and my house, we will serve the Lord. Take some time today and think about the stand you have made in your household. Is it understood that your house serves the Lord?

Lord, lead my family and me to put you first and serve you.

January 30

NOT WHERE I'M FROM BUT WHERE I'M GOING

"Now Jephthah the Gileadite was a mighty man of valor, but he was the son of a harlot; and Gilead begot Jephthah."

Judges 1:1

In college, we identified people by where they were from. Not only that, I learned that people identified themselves by where they were from also, and the descriptions did not always match. For instance, I said people were from Montgomery, Alabama and they stated that they were from "The Gump." I said people were from Birmingham, Alabama and they would reply they were from "Fairfield" or "Pelham" or "Pell City." I would say I was from "H-town" and others would say I was from Huntsville. Almost always, our perception of where we are from does not match what others perceive of where we are from. Jephthah found himself in a similar situation. His view of where he was from did not match the view others (including his half- brothers) had of where he was from. See Jephthah was the son of a prostitute. His brothers ridiculed him for not being a son of their mother. Like Jephthah, we often have no control over where we are from. We do not control the circumstances of our beginnings. However, with God in our lives, we can go in an entirely different direction. No matter where we begin, poor, uneducated, divorced, barren, unemployed—it doesn't matter. What is important is where we are going with Jesus.

Lord, let me not be ashamed of my beginnings, whatever they are. Let me be ever mindful of where you are leading me.

January 31
TOO HOLY FOR ME

"You shall therefore be holy, for I am holy."

Leviticus 11:45b

So many Christians are afraid of the word *holy*. We have allowed the world to place such a negative connotation on the word. We associate it with being religiously proud and haughty. We ridicule dedicated disciples by calling them *holy, holy, holy roller* or *high and mighty*. We criticize their praise by saying, *it doesn't take all that.* Well, according to the Word of God, it takes *all that* and *then some*. We are instructed to *be holy*, just as God is holy. Now our God is perfect in holiness. Did you catch that? Perfect. We are to strive to live a life that is holy and acceptable unto God. Regardless of what others say or think. Often, we associate holiness with the clothes we wear. Many believe that in order for a woman to be holy, she must wear long skirts and cover her arms. Some believe that in order for a man to be holy, he must wear suits all the time. Contrary to popular belief, holiness goes deeper than our attire. Holiness requires a change of attitude, dedication to God, using our gifts, honoring God with our giving, and an active life of prayer and study. If we are committed to these things, holiness will follow.

Lord, let me be holy just as you are holy, regardless to what others say or think. Let me be more concerned with your requirements than the world's standards.

FEBRUARY

February 1
Encourage Yourself

"And David was greatly distressed, for the people spoke of stoning him because the soul of all the people was grieved, every man for his sons and for his daughters; but David encouraged himself in the Lord his God."

1 Samuel 30:6 (KJV21)

While God has put us on this earth to uplift and encourage each other, sometimes, we find ourselves in situations in which we must encourage ourselves. This is especially true for those whom God has called to lead others. In these moments of despair, we must not allow ourselves to get frustrated with the lack of encouragement from others. We must go into our secret place and seek God's presence for encouragement. We must be careful not to become so reliable on the encouragement of man, that we fail to seek the encouragement of God. The truth of the matter is, we all have bad days. Sometimes, tragedy may hit us at the same time as it hits those we are close to. Sometimes, those closest to us can be the ones who hurt or discourage us. In these moments, seek God. Lay your burdens at His feet and know that He cares for you. Be assured that He can give your heart a peace that surpasses all understanding.

Lord, when I am discouraged, let me find encouragement in you and your word.

February 2
GREAT GRACE

"So David said to him, "Do not fear, for I will surely show you kindness for Jonathan your father's sake, and will restore to you all the land of Saul your grandfather; and you shall eat bread at my table continually."

2 Samuel 9:7

I am a woman with a huge heart. One of the reasons I have a huge heart is because I saw my parents model great grace unto others. As a child, I often saw my parents extending grace upon grace upon grace to family and friends, neighbors and strangers. If it were within their power to assist, they would. Being gracious is in direct opposition to what the world tells us. The world says take care of home and look out for yourself. This is in direct opposition to what the Bible teaches us. Take the example found in the key verse. David, the king, extended kindness to his dead best friend's son. Now he didn't know the man, but because of the grace shown to David by his best friend Jonathan, he extended the same loving kindness to his son. This is just a glimpse of God's grace to us. Like Jonathan's son, we were crippled by sin and helpless. But along came the King of Kings who extended grace to us. Now we can fellowship with the King daily because of the great grace He extended to us.

Lord, let me extend to others the great grace you have extended to me.

February 3
STANDING ON MY HIGH "HILLS"

"He makes my feet like the feet of deer, And sets me on my high places."

Psalm 18:33

It is a rare occasion that I am not wearing high heel shoes. In fact, even my tennis shoes have some height to them! I work in a professional office, so I wear heels to work Monday through Friday, to worship most Sundays, and even occasionally on Saturday. Something is empowering about standing in high heels. I am not the tallest person in the world (about 5'2 on a good day), so heels give me a little-added confidence as well as keep my pants legs from dragging the ground. It takes a certain amount of poise and confidence to stand in high heels. The fellas reading this book may not be able to relate to this, however, the same is true about the "high hills" of God. Before God places us in hilltop or mountaintop experiences, He does as the psalmist states in the key verse. He "makes our feet like the feet of deer," that is sure-footed and steady. Once our footing has been steadied in prayer, worship, and study of his word, then He lets us stand on our "high hills." We can then be confident that we will not fall. How pleasant it is to stand in confidence on our high hills.

Lord, grant me to stand in confidence on the "high hills" you place me on.

February 4
NO F.E.A.R.

"The Lord is my light and my salvation; Whom shall I fear? The Lord is the strength of my life; Of whom shall I be afraid?"

Psalm 27:1

With all that is going on in our nation and our world, fear would seem to be the natural response. Wars and rumors of wars, racism, injustice, intolerance, bigotry, sexism, classism will lead us to a pit of despair if we allow it to do so. The natural world has been a mess ever since sin entered the scene. We do not operate in the natural but the supernatural. In times of fear, we find strength and encouragement in the word of God. In the dark places of life, the Lord is our light. When we can't save ourselves, God is our salvation. Even when we are without strength, the Lord is our strength. So what or whom shall we fear?

Lord, I am not afraid because you are my light, my salvation, and my strength.

February 5
BENEFITS OF BELIEVING

"Bless the Lord, O my soul, And forget not all His benefits:"

Psalm 103:2

Too often we become overwhelmed with the responsibility of being a believer. Sometimes it is worth our while to name some of the benefits of being a believer simply. Doing so will encourage us in our walk. The psalmist makes it clear that there are benefits to being a believer. Those benefits include forgiveness of sin, healing of our diseases, redemption from destruction, loving kindness and mercies, righteousness, and justice for the oppressed. Then there are the tangible benefits: a roof over our head, food on the table, jobs, cars to ride in, and friends and family to give us love. We have benefits! Praise God for that!

Lord, let me never forget all the benefits that I have by being your child.

February 6
MY PART

"What can I offer the Lord for all he has done for me? I will lift up the cup of salvation and praise the Lord's name for saving me."
Psalm 116:12-13 (NLT)

There are several gospel songs I love that express the joy of salvation. One says, "When I think about the Lord, how He saved me, how He raised me, how He filled me with the Holy Ghost how He healed me to the uttermost..." and another says, "A wonderful change has come over me..." and a third says, "Jesus is the best thing that ever happened to me..." But we must move beyond joy. Salvation should move us to action. The Psalmist asks the question, "What can I offer God for all he has done for me?" Consider that question. First, what has God done for us? A better question may be, what hasn't God done for us? The answer is give God praise and glory for the wonderful gift of salvation we have been given.

Lord, I will praise you for the indescribable gift of salvation.

February 7
F.R.O.G.

"Trust in the Lord with all your heart, And lean not on your own understanding; In all your ways acknowledge Him, And He shall direct your paths."

Proverbs 3:5-6

Facebook can bring some inspiring things across your timeline. One of the first things someone posted on my timeline was from my big sister in Christ. It was a cartoon of a waving frog with the words "Faithfully Relying On God" underneath. I have also seen the acronym F.R.O.G. stand for Fully Relying On God. Either way, how does a Christian move toward firm and eventually, full reliance on God? The Psalmist offers guidance. First, we must trust God with all our heart and lean not to our own understanding. We need to acknowledge God in all our ways. Finally, we need to be led by the Lord. If we do these things, we can then fully and faithfully rely on God.

Lord, let me fully and faithfully rely on you each day.

February 8

LOOSE LIPS

"The more you talk, the more likely you will cross the line and say the wrong thing; but if you are wise, you'll speak less and with restraint."

Proverbs 10:19 (VOICE)

During World War II, a phrase was created by the War Advertising Council. It was used on posters to describe unguarded talk. The phrase "loose lips sink ships" has been used on many occasions to remind us to be mindful of the words we speak. My children have a catchy little song they sing to remind them as well, *"Be careful little mouth what you say, be careful little mouth what you say, there's a father up above, looking down on you in love, so be careful little mouth what you say."* Indeed, we should be mindful of the words we say. Not just verbally, but also the words we text, tweet, post, and share.

The Bible tells us that the more we talk, the more likely we will cross the line by saying the wrong thing. However, if we are wise, we will speak less and with restraint. Loose lips may sink ships, but wise words make boats float.

Lord, guard my lips and let me be careful with my words. May my words always build up and never tear down.

February 9
FRENEMY

"A friend loves at all times,"

Proverbs 17:17a

The OJs said, "They're smiling in your face all the time trying to take your place." Jill Scott said, "Hate on me hater, now or later. "And TLC said, "What about your friends? Are they gonna be lowdown? Will they ever be around? Or will they turn their backs on you?" Whether you call them backstabbers, haters, or fair weather friends, they are all the same. Sometimes they are friends, and sometimes enemies also known as frenemies. The Urban Dictionary defines "frenemy" as the type of 'friend' whose words or actions bring you down (whether you realize it as intentional or not). When we ask ourselves is that person my friend or enemy, they are your frenemy. They will continue to bring you down until you demand better for yourself. The Bible gives us a clear definition of what a true friend is. It is one who loves at all time. They love you "whether good or bad, happy or sad." We need to make distinctions between friends and enemies. A person cannot be both. They either love us or they don't. They either want the best for us or they don't. They are walking with us or they are not. They are praying for us or against us. We will know they are Christian friends by their love.

Lord, let me have friends that love me and let me be a friend that loves them.

February 10
RETAIL TREACHERY NOT THERAPY
"The rich rule over the poor, and the borrower is slave to the lender."

Proverbs 22:7 (NIV)

The world has tricked us into believe that retail therapy is a great way to relieve stress. We are all guilty of making purchases so we can feel better. While there is nothing wrong with purchasing things for ourselves from time to time, this is not okay when we cannot afford it. Side Note: Just because the money is in your account does not mean you can afford to spend in on shopping! As a result, many have gotten credit cards and even loans to support this "therapy." We feel great and relieved until the credit card bill rolls around or it's time to pay back the loan. In Proverbs, we are advised to be lenders, not borrowers. To be a borrower is to be enslaved by the system, persons, or institutions that loan the money. Let us live comfortably and content. Let us learn to delay gratification rather than growing debt. Let us be lenders and not borrowers. Most importantly, let us find healthy ways to relieve stress. The Bible tells us to bring our trouble to him, not to the closest mall. In order to be the wealthy people God has purposed us to be, we must be wise in our spending and refrain from conforming to the ways of this world.

Lord, lead me to resist the temptation to live beyond my means and let me focus on delaying gratification rather than growing my debt.

February 11
A LAUGHING MATTER

"Blessed are you who hunger now, For you shall be filled. Blessed are you who weep now, For you shall laugh."

Luke 6:21

One of the most beautiful and beneficial things in life is laughter. Medicine has even cited the health benefits of laughter. Research has found that laughter can relieve pain, boost the immune system, reduce blood pressure, stimulate the mind, and burn calories! Laughter also has been found to relieve stress by stimulating organs, soothing tension, and improving your mood. There are spiritual benefits to laughter as well. Laughter and humor are gifts from God. Even in the midst of our storms, we can laugh because we know that God promises in His word to turn our tears of sorrow into tears of laughter. When you are going through difficult moments, challenge yourself to think about something hilarious and let out a huge laugh!

Lord, allow me to laugh at the days to come knowing what you have already done for me in the past.

February 12
GOD DOESN'T CARE ABOUT THAT

But the Lord said to Samuel, "Do not look at his appearance or at his physical stature, because I have refused him. For the Lord does not see as man sees; for man looks at the outward appearance, but the Lord looks at the heart."

1 Samuel 16:17

The world places great emphasis on outward appearances especially when it comes to the clothes we wear and the shoes on our feet. The world has a way of making us feel bad if we aren't wearing the latest designer threads. Unfortunately, many Christians get caught up in being clothed in name brands. God makes it clear in this scripture that He could care less about our outward appearance. He doesn't care about what we look like, his greatest concern is what our hearts look like! So before we shell out thousands of dollars to dress the part for the world, let us pay close attention to the posture of our hearts! There's absolutely nothing wrong with wanting to look nice and fashionable, however, this desire must not take precedence over the condition of our hearts.

Lord, help me to become more concerned with how my heart looks to you rather than how my outward appearance appears to the world.

February 13
ALL I HAVE IS WHAT I KNOW

"Your word I have hidden in my heart, that I might not sin against You."

Psalm 119:11

Life comes at us quickly. Many situations in life do not allow us time to pull out our physical Bible or tap the Bible app on our phone. Sometimes, the only word we have is the word within us. All we have is what we know. We, therefore, have to be able to pull the word up whenever we need it. In our scripture for today, the Psalmist advises us to hide the word of God in our hearts to keep us from sin. In order to hide it, we must study it daily. Challenge yourself to learn a few verses "by heart" that you can pull out in times of trouble.

Lord, let us hide the word in our hearts so that it keeps us from sin.

February 14
SOUL FRIENDS

"Two are better than one, because they have a good return for their labor: If either of them falls down, one can help the other up. But pity anyone who falls and has no one to help them up. Also, if two lie down together, they will keep warm. But how can one keep warm alone? Though one may be overpowered, two can defend themselves. A cord of three strands is not quickly broken."

Ecclesiastes 4: 9-12 (NIV)

The Urban dictionary defines a Soul Friend as better than any friend; you've known them so long, and so well you might as well be family. Oxford defines Soul Friend as a person whose thoughts, feelings and attitudes closely match those of another; kindred spirit; the sibling we got to choose. As Christians, we should seek "Soul Friends." Christians of like mind, focus, and souls. A Soul Friend helps us up when we have fallen. They encourage us to repent and get back up again. They keep our souls warm during the cold periods of life. Most of all, they are a praying friend. Thank God for Soul Friends.

Lord, give me Soul Friends of like mind, focus, and souls.

February 15
JOY-FULL, PEACE-FULL

"Now may the God of hope fill you with all joy and peace as you believe in Him so that you may overflow with hope by the power of the Holy Spirit."

Romans 15:13 (HCSB)

The joy that I have, the world didn't give it to me. This peace that I have, the world didn't give it to me. This hope that I have, the world didn't give it to me. The world didn't give it, the world can't take it away." If you've been to church or around some church goers, I'm sure you've heard this song a few times. The words of this song speaks to the truth of Romans 15:13. When we put our hope in God, by the power of the Holy Spirit, we will be filled. We will be hopeful. We will be joyful. We will be peaceful. Our belief in God fills us with unspeakable joy, the peace that passes all understanding and overflowing with hope all by the power of the Holy Spirit. We must protect this peace, joy, and hope. We cannot allow the conditions and circumstances of this world to taint this God-given joy, peace, and hope. We must protect it at all costs!

Lord, grant me your joy, peace that passes all understanding, and hopes that overflows.

February 16
MORE THAN LIP SERVICE

"Therefore the Lord said: "Inasmuch as these people draw near with their mouth, and honor Me with their lips, but have removed their hearts far from Me, and their fear toward Me is taught by the commandment of men."

Isaiah 29:13

One writer said, "We cannot call ourselves Christians and live in direct opposition to what we claim to be." As Christians, we talk a good a good talk, but often fail at walking the walk. This is hypocrisy. People would rather see a sermon than just hear a sermon. We must remind ourselves daily that we may be the only Bible some people read and the only Jesus some people ever see. God wants our lips and our lives. We should honor him with our lips and our lives. It's about life service, not just lip service. Strive to always live a life that reveals Christ.

Lord, let me always honor you with my lips and my life.

February 17
GOD OF MY TEARS

"Depart from me, all evildoers, for the LORD has heard the sound of my weeping. The LORD has heard my plea for help; the LORD accepts my prayer."

Psalm 6: 8-9 (HCSB)

Some of life's situations hit us so hard that they rock us to our core and render us speechless. Some situations in life lead us to tears; not the corner of our eye-dabbing, softly sniffing tears, but the weeping, chest heaving, runny nose tears. This world will cause you to weep, but there is an encouraging word from the Lord when we are speechless and weeping. God, in His infinite wisdom, understands the prayers in our tears. He hears the whispers in our weeping. God hears our requests and receives our prayers. Our God is so loving and near, He hears those prayers we sow in tears.

Lord, hear my prayers, those I say with my lips and those I say with my tears.

February 18
PLEASURE PRINCIPAL

"And even when you ask, you don't get it because your motives are all wrong—you want only what will give you pleasure."

James 4:3 (NLT)

Too often we are driven by pleasure. We allow our flesh to control our thoughts and actions rather than the Holy Spirit. The world says, if it feels good, do it. If it tastes good, eat it. If it looks good, buy it. If it sounds good, believe it. We must guard against pleasure being the priority. James tells us that we ask for the wrong things because we are pleasure driven. Janet Jackson called it the "Pleasure Principle." When we are driven by pleasure, it messes up our prayer life because we will ask out of wrong motives. You can see this happening when our prayers become more selfish. At that point, we must acknowledge, repent, and refocus.

Lord, let my motives be pure and not out of pleasure when I pray.

February 19
SOMETHING NEW

"Behold, I am doing a new thing; now it springs forth, do you not perceive it?"

Isaiah 43:19a (HCSB)

Bill Keane said, "Yesterday is history, tomorrow is a mystery, today is a gift of God, which is why we call it the present." Yesterday is history—you can't get back the stones you've thrown, the words you've spoken, occasions you've missed, time that is gone, or trust you've lost. Tomorrow—who knows besides God? What we do have is the present—a gift from God. With each present moment, we have the opportunity for God to do something new in our lives if we allow him to. Our bodies were designed with the future in mind. We face forward, and all our anatomy is a forward design. Let us, therefore, stand surefooted in the present, while stepping out into the new things God will do in our future.

Lord, do a new thing in my life. Let it spring forth and don't let me miss it.

February 20
PAID IN FULL

"But he was wounded for our transgressions, he was bruised for our iniquities; upon him was the chastisement that made us whole, and with his stripes we are healed."

Isaiah 53:5

Ricky Dillard summarizes the great debt Jesus paid on our behalf in "Because of the Blood." He states, "He paid the debt that He did not owe, what came from His hands, His feet, and His side, was more precious than silver and gold, the blood that set me free, I know it saves me from a life-ending tragedy. Now I'm born again free from sin because of the blood." The hymn writer said, "Years I spent in vanity and pride, caring not my Lord was crucified, knowing not it was for me He died, at Calvary. Mercy there was great, and grace was free. Pardon, there was multiplied to me. There my burdened soul found liberty, at Calvary." What great debt our transgressions and iniquities accumulated. Oh, but the blood of Jesus! It paid the debt in our stead. It bought our liberty, it gave us mercy and grace, and it healed our sin-sick souls. Thank God our debt has been paid in full.

Lord, thank you for paying the debt you did not owe. What a great sacrifice you made on our behalf.

February 21
Exchange

"To console those who mourn in Zion, to give them beauty for ashes, the oil of joy for mourning, the garment of praise for the spirit of heaviness..."

Isaiah 61:3

Two of the greatest pains I have ever felt occurred in 2007; when I lost my mom and miscarried our first baby. My heart felt like it was breaking apart...but God! I was encouraged by the words of Isaiah that says God gives beauty for ashes, strength for tears, joy for mourning, and praise for heaviness. I especially like the VOICE translation that says, "As for those who grieve over Zion, God has sent me to give them a beautiful crown in exchange for ashes, to anoint them with gladness instead of sorrow, to wrap them in victory, joy, and praise instead of depression and sadness." How wonderful it is to know that our God will take the most painful, ugly, mournful, and heavy times of our life and turn them into beauty, strength, joy, and praise!

Lord, let me remember in times of pain, problems, and tears that you will give me beauty, strength, and joy.

February 22
YOUTH IS NO EXCUSE

"But the Lord said to me: "Do not say, 'I am a youth, for you shall go to all to whom I send you, and whatever I command you, you shall speak,"

Jeremiah 1:7

When did you accept Christ as Lord and Savior? Were you a child, a teen, a young adult, or a grown up? Many Christians that accept Christ as children or teens struggle to walk in the gifts God gave them. I accepted Christ at the age of eight. The love of Christ has always been around me. I have always wanted to be close to God. But youthful enthusiasm is not always received with the same enthusiasm. However, being youthful is not an excuse. We need to run for Jesus, go where he says go and say what he says to say whether we are a child, a teen, or a grown up. God called Jeremiah at a young age. He used him just as he had used people who were older than him. Regardless of your age, don't hinder how God desires to use you.

Lord, do not allow my age to be an excuse for not going, doing and saying whatever it is you would have me to do or say.

February 23
NEW MERCY

"It is of the Lord's mercies that we are not consumed, because his compassions fail not. They are new every morning: great is thy faithfulness."
Lamentations 3:22-23 (KJV)

love early morning. That is my designated time of devotion. I try to wake each morning a few minutes before I have to get up to spend some quiet time with the Lord. Before the hustle and bustle of the day begin, I take a few minutes to read the word, read a devotional, and pray. One of the first things I do is praise God for another day he has allowed me to see. Why? Because as the CEV translation said so plainly, "Then I remember something that fills me with hope. The Lord's kindness never fails! If he had not been merciful, we would have been destroyed. The Lord can always be trusted to show mercy each morning." Wow! God is always kind, if not for his kindness shown in mercy, we would all be destroyed. The Bible doesn't say punished, hurt, or wounded; it says destroyed! Because of the mercy of God (not getting what we really deserve, God saying no when he could have said yes) we are not destroyed. Not only that, we receive new mercy every morning! I just love the morning.

Lord, thank you for your mercy that is new every morning and more than that, it is because of it that we are not destroyed.

February 24
PLANNED TO PROSPER

"For I know the plans I have for you," declares the Lord, "plans to prosper you and not to harm you, plans to give you hope and a future."

Jeremiah 29:11 (NIV)

The dictionary defines prosperity as the state of being prosperous; success, profitability, affluence, wealth, opulence, luxury, the good life, milk, and honey, (good) fortune, ease, plenty, comfort, security, well-being. The "prosperity gospel" has gained popularity among Christians in recent years. It focuses on material wealth blessings, "name it and claim it," and minimal emphasis on sin. It presents wealth as a sign of God's favor. However, the Bible tells us that prosperity comes from God's plans for our lives. His plans are not to harm us, but to give us a hope and a future. We need to guard our hearts and minds against the trick of the enemy to shift focus from God and his plans to prosper us to his plans to make us focus on material prosperity.

Lord, let me keep you focus on your plans to prosper to us and not gaining material prosperity.

February 25
MY BODY MY TEMPLE

"Do you not know that your bodies are temples of the Holy Spirit, who is in you, whom you have received from God? You are not your own."

1 Corinthians 6:19

From the early days of computer programming the phrase "garbage in, garbage out" means whatever we put in, will come out. The same is true with our mind, body, and soul. Whatever we place into our minds, our bodies, and our souls affects us. If we pollute our minds with negative ungodly thoughts; if we treat our bodies as our own and do whatever whenever with whomever; if we fail to pray, study, worship, give, and serve God, we threaten to put garbage in and get garbage out. The opposite is also true. If we recognize that our bodies are temples of the Holy Spirit and we should treat them as such. We should guard our minds with godly thoughts and the mind of Christ; we should treat our bodies as the temple of the Lord that it is, not ours to do whatever whenever with whomever we want; we should consistently pray, study, worship, give and serve God—then we are treating our bodies as temples.

Lord, let me honor my temple mind, body, and soul.

February 26
TALKING LOUD SAYING NOTHING

*"holding to a form of [outward] godliness (religion), although they
have denied its power [for their conduct nullifies their claim of
faith]. Avoid such people and keep far away from them."*

2 Timothy 3:5 (AMP)

Many people join church, but fail to accept God as Lord and Savior. They claim to be believers in public, but they don't act like believers in private. Outwardly, they appear holy in righteous, but inwardly, they do not honor or reverence the ways of God. We can tell from the way they talk and how they treat people. The Bible tells us to avoid such people. Knowing "church talk" and church procedures does not mean that we are Christians. There is a difference in our lips and lives. "Form of godliness" is to be good, to like other people, and to be selfish where "Godly" is to be like God, love others, and to be selfless. Be sure that your lip service to God matches your life service. Don't just talk about being a Christian! You must live like one as well!

**Lord, let make sure my walk matches my talk and that my life
is in relationship with you**

February 27
WRITE IT DOWN

"And then God answered: "Write this. Write what you see. Write it out in big block letters so that it can be read on the run. This vision-message is a witness pointing to what's coming. It aches for the coming—it can hardly wait! And it doesn't lie. If it seems slow in coming, wait. It's on its way. It will come right on time."
Habakkuk 2:2-3 (MSG)

There is power in the written word. Even research has shown the advantages of writing down dreams and goals. The written word captures our thoughts, ideas, and dreams. Greg Reid said, "A dream written down with a date becomes a goal; a goal broken down into steps becomes a plan; a plan backed by action makes your dreams come true." He echoes the words of a familiar Biblical passage where we are encouraged to write the vision that God has given us. When we write something down, we tend to remember it long afterward. It makes the thought, idea, or dream more tangible. It moves us, through the power of God, to move our dreams and visions to action.

Lord, let me write down what you have placed in me so that I can take action guided by you.

February 28
READ. PRAY. SLAY.

"They read out of the book of the law of God, translating and giving the meaning so that the people could understand what was read."

Nehemiah 8:8 (HCSB)

READ. Take time to read the scripture daily. Allow God to speak to you. Ask yourself, "What is God saying?" Write the scripture down in a journal or your Bible, highlight, underline, and make notes in margins of anything that stands out. Reread the scripture. Ask yourself how can you apply the scripture to your daily life.

P.R. A.Y. Praise God for who He is and what He has done. Listen to some devotional music. Read some scriptures of praise. Repent. Confess your sins to God so that they will not hinder your prayers. Turn from any sin you have been practicing. Ask God to reveal any hidden sin. Ask. Tell God all your concerns. Leave them all at the altar. Yield. Believe that God has heard and is answering your prayer.

S.L. A.Y.—Seek the Lord and Yield. Chase God and the things of God in every aspect of your life. Seek His will in all you do. Accept God as Savior and LORD of your life. Give Him Lordship over every area of your life. Continually ask yourself what God's word says about situations. You have read and prayed, now submit to God's will and yield.

Lord, help me to daily Read, Pray, and Slay.

MARCH

March 1
PRAY FOR US

"Finally, our friends, please pray for us. This will help the message about the Lord to spread quickly, and others will respect it, just as you do."

2 Thessalonians 3:1a

What do you do when someone asks you to pray for them? Do you say you will and never do? Do you say a quick prayer but fail to follow through? Prayer is an important discipline in the life of a Christian. More importantly, as our prayer life matures we will find ourselves praying for others more than ourselves. Try this, the next time someone asks you to pray for them, do so right then and there. Praise God for the opportunity to pray. Repent of any sins that may hinder your prayer from being answered. Ask God to meet the needs of the person you are praying for. Yield to God's will in every situation.

Lord, let me never miss an opportunity to pray for others.

START WITH SUBMISSION

"Therefore submit to God. Resist the devil and he will flee from you."

James 4:7

As a young academic in the field of science, I had been encouraged to be assertive, independent, and self-reliant. Unfortunately, those attitudes carried over into my personal as well as spiritual life. When it comes to our relationship with God, we must be submitted to his will and his way for our lives. Submission doesn't always feel good, but it is most definitely for our good! When we submit to God, we gain the strength we need to endure the attacks hell sends our way. Sometimes, submitting to God's will may require us to turn down jobs, relationships, and other opportunities that we desire. Today, I encourage you to submit to God, regardless of what it looks like. He knows our end and our beginning. He can see into our futures much further than we can. When we submit to him in our "right now", we can rest assured that though we may not understand, it will definitely benefit us in the long run!

Lord, grant me a willing spirit to submit unto you.

March 3

GREAT MERCY, GREAT LOVE

"But God, being [so very] rich in mercy, because of His great and wonderful love with which He loved us, "

Ephesians 2:4 (AMP)

What we deserved was death. The Bible is obvious on the consequences of sin. *The wages of sin is death; the soul that sins it shall surely die...*But God. Mercy is not getting what we deserve. The dictionary defines mercy as compassion or forgiveness is shown toward someone whom it is within one's power to punish or harm. Mercy is direct opposition to how the enemy would have us behave. Where there is great love, there is great mercy. God's mercy flows directly from his love for us.

Lord, thank you for not giving me what I truly deserve.

March 4
I KNOW WHO I AM

When the world distracts us and tries to define who we are, we need to look no further than the word of God to remind ourselves of who we are and whose we are." Today, read the following scriptures to understand and remind yourself of your identity in Christ!

"I am alive with Christ."
Ephesians 2:5 (NKJV)
"I am free from the law of sin and death."
Romans 8:2 (NKJV)
"I am holy and without blame before Him in love."
Ephesians 1:4; 1 Peter 1:16 (NKJV)
"I am God's workmanship, created in Christ unto good works."
Ephesians 2:10 (NKJV)
"I am a new creature in Christ."
2 Corinthians 5:17 (NKJV)
"I am a joint-heir with Christ."
Romans 8:17 (NKJV)
"I am more than a conqueror through Him Who loves me."
Romans 8:37 (NKJV)
"I am an overcomer by the blood of the Lamb and the word of my testimony."
Revelation 12:11 (NKJV)
"I am an ambassador for Christ."
2 Corinthians 5:20 (NKJV)
"I am forgiven of all my sins and washed in the Blood."
Ephesians 1:7 (NKJV)
"I am healed by the stripes of Jesus."
Isaiah 53:5; 1 Peter 2:24 (NKJV)

Lord, remind me daily who I am and whose I am.

March 5

I PUT OFF, I PUT ON

"that you put off, concerning your former conduct, the old man which grows corrupt according to the deceitful lusts, and be renewed in the spirit of your mind, and that you put on the new man which was created according to God, in true righteousness and holiness."

Ephesians 4:22-24

Today, take some time to evaluate if you have put off the old man and put on the new person you are in God!

- Put on Salvation: *Am I saved? Have I truly accepted Jesus Christ into my heart?*
- Put on the Lord: *Is Jesus the Lord of my life? Can others see Christ in my life?*
- Put on the Word of God: *Do I own a Bible? Do I study it daily?*
- Put on Prayer: *Do I P.R.A.Y. (Praise, Repent, Ask, Yield) daily? Often?*
- Put on a church home: *Do I have a church home where I attend on a regular basis?*
- Put on your spiritual gifts: *Do I know what my spiritual gifts are? Do I operate in them?*
- Put on ministry: *Do I participate in ministry inside and outside of my church home?*
- Put on godly friendships: *Do I have godly friendships?*
- Put on study: *Do I participate in regular Bible study outside of Sunday Morning Worship?*
- Put on good stewardship: *Do I glorify God with my finances? Do I tithe?*
- Put on witnessing: *Do I share Christ with others on a regular basis?*

Lord, let me put off the old man and put on the new man.

March 6
PRAISE THE LORD

"Let everything that has breath praise the Lord. Praise the Lord."
Psalm 150:6 (NIV)

The Bible instructs *everyone* and *everything* to praise the Lord. Who? *Everything* that has breath! All people and all creation! Humans and animals inhale oxygen and exhale carbon dioxide (breath). Plants inhale carbon dioxide and exhale oxygen (breath). What? *Praise the Lord!* Where? *Everywhere!* When? *Forever!* Why? *His acts and abundant greatness.* How? Worship *with instruments, dance, clapping, raising hands, and singing.* "Let everything that breathes praise the Lord!" When we develop a relationship with the Lord, we can't help but worship Him.

Lord, you're worthy of all the glory and all the honor and all the praise

March 7
CHANGE YOUR MIND

"For "who has known the mind of the Lord that he may instruct Him?" But we have the mind of Christ."

1 Corinthians 2:16

Our perspective on things is essential. It has been said that if you can change your mind, you can your life and change starts in the mind. The mind of Christ changes our view of everything. When we trivialize the things of God, it is easy to be disobedient. Skip church, don't read your Bible, fail to pray—no big deal. But when we have the mind of Christ, it changes everything. With the mind of Christ, we regularly attend not only worship service, but also Bible study and Sunday School. We diligently read our Bibles to fill our minds with truth and to take captive our thoughts. We are persistent in prayer. Then we begin to strengthen our bonds with godly friends and allow them to hold us accountable. Ultimately, having the mind of Christ leads us into closer fellowship with Jesus the Christ. We will wake up each morning with our mind on Jesus. We will have the mind of Christ.

Lord, change my mind and give me the mind of Christ.

March 8
I DON'T DO CHURCH

*"not giving up meeting together, as some are in the habit of
doing, but encouraging one another—and all the more as you
see the Day approaching."*

Hebrews 10:25

Let me be transparent for a moment. I don't go to church
anymore. I do not attend church. I am not a church member.
I have stopped giving money to the church, and I don't do
anything at church anymore. I don't do church. I go to worship. I
am no longer a church attendee; I attend worship service. I am not
a church member, but a member of the body of Christ. I don't give
money to church anymore either, I now tithe and give to edify the
body of Christ. I don't do anything at church anymore. I serve in
ministry. As I said, I don't do church anymore. Do you?

**Lord, let me not do church anymore and focus on being the
church.**

March 9
UGLY PRODUCE

"Now the works of the flesh are evident, which are: adultery, fornication, uncleanness, lewdness, idolatry, sorcery, hatred, contentions, jealousies, outbursts of wrath, selfish ambitions, dissensions, heresies, envy, murders, drunkenness, revelries, and the like; of which I tell you beforehand, just as I also told you in time past, that those who practice such things will not inherit the kingdom of God. But the fruit of the Spirit is love, joy, peace, longsuffering, kindness, goodness, faithfulness, gentleness, self-control. Against such there is no law."

Galatians 5:19-23

As a measure to reduce food waste, many grocery stores are embracing "ugly produce." Ugly produce is the fruit and vegetables that are not aesthetically pleasing, but taste just like the "prettier" produce. As Christians, we sometimes yield "ugly produce" as well. This is the work of the flesh. The Message translation warns us about behaviors such as repetitive, loveless, cheap sex; a stinking accumulation of mental and emotional garbage; frenzied and joyless grabs for happiness. We are advised to walk in the Spirit and produce the fruit of the spirit. There is nothing ugly about spiritual produce.

Lord, let me walk daily in the Spirit, so I do not practice the works of the flesh.

March 10

FREEDOM

"And you shall know the truth, and the truth shall make you free."
John 8:32 (NKJV)

Harriett Tubman said, "I freed a thousand slaves I could have freed a thousand more if only they knew they were slaves." Unfortunately, the cruel institution of slavery stripped millions of people of their humanity. More than that, they were led to believe that their only status in life was that of slave. Many Christians are walking around believing that they are free, but they are really in bondage. They are enslaved to people, relationships, careers, desires, and feelings. They are still bound to sin. If only they knew they were enslaved.

Christ has set us free! It is knowledge of the truth of Jesus Christ that sets us free. The good news is that if Jesus has set us free, we are truly free! No longer shackled by sin and shame, we are free. Now walk in that freedom.

Lord, help me to remember that I am free in Jesus Christ, no more bondage, I am free.

March 11
GOD IS ABLE

"Now to Him who is able to do exceedingly abundantly above all that we ask or think, according to the power that works in us,"
Ephesians 3:20 (NKJV)

Where some would call me hopelessly optimistic; those who truly know me would call me a hopeful optimistic. H.O.P.E.—having only positive expectations is possible only because God is able. It isn't that God is just able; He is able to do exceedingly abundantly, above all, superabundantly, immeasurably more, awe-inspiring things, immeasurable things. But more than that, He is able to do above and beyond what we ask, think, imagine, dream, hope, or pray! This is a certainty that when my limited power can't, God's unlimited power can. The Holy Spirit constantly reminds us that God IS able. When you experience situations that are beyond your own control, turn them over to God! Rest assured that He can handle them far better than you can.

Lord, remind me daily that you are able to do exceedingly abundantly above and beyond all that I can ask, think, imagine, hope, dream, or pray for.

March 12
WORRY TO WORSHIP

"Be anxious for nothing, but in everything by prayer and supplication, with thanksgiving, let your requests be made known to God;"

Philippians 4:6 (NKJV)

I wrestle with worry. I worry about my husband, children, family, and my friends. I worry about my church, city, nation, and our world. I worry about my health, career, and my future. I have always been this way, ever since I was a child. I believe worry is a negative side effect of being an encourager. There is a thin line between encouragement and worry. Often, I end up worrying about the very people I am supposed to be encouraging. As a professional worrier, I have learned to turn worry on its head by worshiping when I start worrying. Worry is repeating to yourself how big your problem or concern is, where worship is repeating to yourself how big and powerful my God is. The Bible admonishes me and all other worriers to not worry about anything but to pray about everything. The power of prayer turns our worry into worship.

Lord, forgive me when I worry and always lead me into worship.

81

March 13
A Real Prayer Life

(AMP) "Be unceasing and persistent in prayer;"
(CEB) "Pray continually."
(CEV) "and never stop praying."
(ERV) "Never stop praying."
(HCSB) "Pray constantly."
(TLB) "Always keep on praying."
(MSG) "pray all the time;"
(NKJV) "pray without ceasing,"

1 Thessalonians 5:17

How on earth can one pray all the time? Our religious views on prayer can sometimes make us believe that it is impossible to pray all the time. Many believe that in order to pray, we must be bent over in a prayer closet and yelling scriptures to God continuously. This can't be further from the truth. Allow me to share a secret with you about prayer. Prayer is communication with the Father. Though it is great to intentionally set aside quiet time alone to commune with God, we can also pray as we are at work and carry out our daily talks. In fact, we should condition our minds to not just have prayer time, but have a prayer life. A prayer life requires us to be in constant communication with God throughout the day. The same way you communicate with your friends throughout the day is the same way God desires us to be in communication with him. You don't have to wait until you get home and put the kids down. You can speak to God in your mind, and in your heart. Understand the simplicity of prayer will allow you to see that you can indeed: Pray without Ceasing!

Lord, let me always have a prayerful mindset.

March 14
AGREE TO BE AGREEABLE

"My dear friends, as a follower of our Lord Jesus Christ, I beg you to get along with each other. Don't take sides. Always try to agree in what you think."

1 Corinthians 1:10 (CEV)

The devil loves division. It is one of his most frequently used tactics, especially within the body of Christ and in particular between Christian. The enemy knows if he plants seeds of doubt and deception in a relationship that he can destroy it. Especially among Christians. He knows that Christian praying friends are the most powerful kind. Paul admonishes us in his letter to the church at Corinth to get along with each other, don't take sides, always be together in what you think.

Lord, let me always be in agreement with others, agreeable, on one accord with no divisions.

March 15
PRAYER POWER

"The prayer of a righteous person is powerful and effective."
James 5:16b (NIV)

Our prayers are powerful and effective if we are righteous. Other translations say "right living." If we want to see our prayers change things or better yet, see our prayers change us, we must live right. We cannot allow anything to hinder our prayers. What are some things that can hinder our prayers? Unforgiven sin can hinder our prayers. Harboring sin in our hearts, the Lord will not hear us. Un-forgiveness can hinder our prayers. The Bible tells us that if we do not forgive others, God will not forgive us. We cannot approach a righteous God when we are living wrong by practicing sin. We do not want anyone or anything to hinder our prayers. We want to be righteous so that our prayers are powerful and effective.

Lord, do not allow me to let anything or anyone hinder my prayers because I want them to be powerful and effective.

March 16
ALL OR NOTHING

"that you may love the Lord your God, that you may obey His voice, and that you may cling to Him, for He is your life and the length of your days;"

Deuteronomy 30:20a

My husband and I have been married for over 13 years. Though it sounds cliché, it does seem like only yesterday. Marriage is a covenant relationship designed by God to be a representation to the world of the covenant relationship He desires to have with each of us through His son Jesus Christ. In covenant relationships, we are asked to love, obey, and cling. Though seemingly simplistic at first glance, deeper reflection reveals that you must do all three or none at all. It all begins with love. When we accept the love of God into our lives, we love the Lord with all our heart, mind, and soul. If we love the Lord, then we will seek to obey Him. Will we always succeed? Of course not! But our goal should always be to obey God. Finally, if we love God and obey him, then we can cling to Him. The term "cling" is referenced several times in the Bible. Cling can be defined as "hold on tightly to or attach oneself to." The only way we can hold tightly to or attach ourselves to God, to cling to Him, is if we love Him and obey Him. It's all or nothing, so cling.

Lord, let me love you, obey you and cling to you with all my heart.

March 17

S.L.A.Y. EVERYDAY

"So submit to [the authority of] God. Resist the devil [stand firm against him] and he will flee from you."

James 4:7 (AMP)

The devil is sly in his approach. He uses life situations to make us believe that we are defeated and our situations will never change. The good news is that the more we read the word of God and pray, the more will come to understand that the devil is the father of lies. The Bible tells us that we are victorious through Christ; we can do all things through Him; no weapon formed against us shall prosper; the latter will be better than the former, but we must first submit to God. Surrender our lives in salvation, yield to the Lordship of Christ and live holy, study the word of God to show ourselves approved, forsake not going to church, be faithful in ministry, use our gifts to the glory of God, and pray all the time. This is a life of submission to the authority of God, surrendered to God, and obedience to God. Then we can resist the enemy, stand against him, fight against him and he will flee.

Lord, let me daily submit to you so that I can resist the devil and he flees.

March 18
NOBODY HAS TIME FOR THAT

"For we do not have a high priest who is unable to empathize with our weaknesses, but we have one who has been tempted in every way, just as we are—yet he did not sin."

Hebrews 4:15 (NIV)

The hymn writer said, "Yield not to temptation, for yielding is sin, each victory will help you or some others to win. Fight manfully onward, dark passions subdue. Look ever to Jesus and He'll carry you through. Just ask the Savior to help you, to comfort, strengthen and keep you. He is willing to aid you. He will carry you through." Our Savior can empathize with our weaknesses because He was tempted in every way we are, but He did not sin. The sin is not in being tempted. The sin is in yielding to the sin. So what can you do? Ask the Savior to help you, comfort you, strengthen you, keep you. Jesus is willing to aid you. He will carry you through. Yielding to temptation—nobody has time for that.

Lord, when temptation rears its ugly head, help me, comfort me, strengthen me, aid me, carry me through.

March 19
SPEAKING TO THE STORM

"They came to Jesus and woke Him, saying, "Master, Master, we are about to die!" He got up and rebuked the wind and the raging, violent waves, and they ceased, and it became calm [a perfect peacefulness]."

Luke 8:24 (AMP)

I have loved the song "I Told the Storm" for years, but I listened with new ears after reading Luke 8:24. The soloist is not *naming it and claiming it*. On the contrary, she is speaking the Word of God to the storm! When the storms of life blow (there is probably a storm blowing in your life right now), we must be equipped before we can tell the storm anything!

Equipping comes from being in right relationship with God. We know when we're walking righteous and when we're walking raggedy. Equipping also comes from confessing our sins. If we harbor unconfessed sin or continue in a sin, we hinder our ability to speak to our storms. Not only that, God will not hear our requests until we repent. Finally, equipping also comes from knowing the Word of God. We cannot speak what we don't know. God's promises are not vain repetitions, but things we know to be true. We should keep some in our spiritual storm kits. Speak to your storms and watch them cease and leave you in perfect peace.

Lord, when the storms of life are blowing remind me to speak to the storm and tell the storm how great my God is, how powerful his promise are, and how perfect his peace is.

March 20
EYES WIDE SHUT

"We live [walk] by what we believe [faith], not by what we can see [sight]."

2 Corinthians 5:7 (EXB)

How do we walk by faith and not by sight? How do we live by what believe and not by what we can see? First, we must have a clear understanding of what faith is. It is "the substance of things hoped for and the evidence of things not seen," (Hebrew 11:1); it is also "calling nonexistent things into existence, (Romans 4:17). Faith is leaping without looking. It is trusting without touching. It is expecting without explanation. It is courage in calamity. It is praying and believing. So how do we walk by faith or live by what we believe? We do it with our eyes wide shut, believing what we can't see and walking where we have no sight.

Lord, strengthen my faith to walk and live by what I believe and not what I see.

March 21
SERENITY

*"And the peace of God, which transcends all understanding,
will guard your hearts and your minds in Christ Jesus"*

Philippians 4:7

The peace of God is different from any peace we will ever experience. Have you ever witnessed someone smiling even though their world has been turned upside down? Sometimes, we see these people and wonder to ourselves, "How on earth are they smiling right now." They are able to smile because God has filled their hearts with a peace that surpasses what they feel and understand. We can have this type of peace no matter what the world throws our way. In Philippians 4, Paul tells us not to be anxious about anything. Instead, he admonishes us to submit our requests to God with thanksgiving. Only then will we be able to experience this type of peace. Today, when situations hit your life unexpectedly, submit your requests to God. Allow Him to sort out everything on your behalf, and grant you a peace that overtakes your understanding of everything going on around you!

Lord, grant me the serenity to accept change and use wisdom.

March 22
THIS IS MY FATHER'S WORLD

"Why do you confuse the issue? Why do you talk without knowing what you're talking about? Where were you when I created the earth? Tell me, since you know so much! Who decided on its size? Certainly you'll know that! Who came up with the blueprints and measurements? How was its foundation poured, and who set the cornerstone,"

Job 38: 2-5 (MSG)

I can remember my grandfather often saying, "This is my father's world." The lyrics to the hymn remind us that every minute detail on earth is under the spiritual care of our heavenly father. *"This is my Father's world, O let me ne'er forget that though the wrong seems oft so strong, God is the ruler yet. This is my Father's world: why should my heart be sad? The Lord is King; let the heavens ring! God reigns; let the earth be glad! This is my Father's world. No matter what comes my way, this is my Father's world."*

No matter what is going on, this is my Father's world. No matter the trials and tribulations, pressures or problems, sin, and stupidity. In spite of my stumbling and my steps. This is my Father's world. I will not worry or fret for this is my Father's world.

Lord, when troubles and trials shake my faith remind me daily that this is my Father's world.

March 23
I LIVE IN HIM

"for in Him we live and move and have our being, as also some of your own poets have said, 'For we are also His offspring.'"

Acts 17:28

We have no life outside of God. God formed us in our mothers' wombs. He made us in His image. It is in Him we live, move, and have our being. One hymn often raised during revival said it this way, "I can't live in this world without the Lord...I can't raise my right hand without the Lord...I can't treat my neighbor right without the Lord...I can't bow on my knees without the Lord...When I look around and see what the Lord has done for me, I can't live in this world without the Lord." Without God, we can't live, move, breathe, think, love, or pray. We cannot do anything with God. We live in Him; He gives us life.

Lord, thank you for allowing me to live, move, and be in you.

March 24

SOURCE OF MY STRENGTH

"The Lord is my strength and my shield; my heart trusted in Him, and I am helped; Therefore my heart greatly rejoices, and with my song I will praise Him."

Psalm 28:7

hen we are without strength physically, emotionally, and spiritually; when we have no power of our own to go on; when we do not have the physical ability to lift our own heads; when the troubles of life weigh us down, the Lord is our strength. When we are being bombarded by the fiery darts of the world, the Lord is our shield… our *impenetrable* shield. We already know what God has done in the past. Therefore, our hearts rejoice and trust in God. All our help comes from God, that gives us reasons to praise. If you find yourself weak, don't be discouraged. Instead, realize that you are in the perfect position for God's strength to be revealed in you and through you.

Lord, thank you for being my strength in weakness, my shield in attack and my help.

March 25

GOT TO TELL IT

"Let the redeemed of the Lord say so, whom He has redeemed from the hand of the enemy,"

Psalm 107:2

When I got serious in my relationship with Christ, I heard the term justification. I often heard people say that we are justified through Christ Jesus. I wondered what that word truly meant. Today, I want to share with you a story that helped me to understand what our justification through Christ truly means.

There once was a man who went out in search for a wife. He knew a very rich man in the next town who had two daughters. He decided to travel there. He gathered six of his best oxen and every piece of silver he had put aside for the last 33 years of his life. He traveled to the rich man's house and made his offer for one of his daughter's hand in marriage. The rich man had already given the beautiful daughter's hand in marriage just before the man arrived. His other daughter, was not as beautiful. In fact, many people felt that this daughter was ugly and worthless. The man thought that surely the rich man would accept a lower gift for this daughter, but the rich man required him to give the same gift he was willing to give for the other daughter. The man agreed and took his wife home.

As he made his way back into his hometown with his wife on top of his horse, the townspeople joked him. "What a foolish man! What will she be worth to you in a few years?"

The man proudly looked up and said, "She was worth everything I had. Her value is not in what she looks like, her value is in what I was willing to give up for her!"

With that, he went home with his wife and they lived happily ever after.

We were redeemed by Jesus Christ! We were worthless, filthy, and destined for hell! However, Jesus Christ came along and paid the ultimate price for our salvation. What we do, the titles we do or do not hold, and our possessions or lack thereof don't give us our value. Our value is in what Jesus Christ paid for us. He thought we were worth his very life! Our redemption and salvation should not be something we hold a secret! The scripture above reminds us that if we have been redeemed, we should say so! We have nothing to be ashamed of! We were bought for a PRICE!

Lord, let me never hesitate to tell of the redemption you made on my behalf.

March 26
DO NOT IGNORE THE PEOPLE FACTOR

"Do not be deceived: "Evil company corrupts good habits."
1 Corinthians 15:33

We must be careful about the company we keep. Sometimes, it can be difficult to determine whether someone is a good friend to us. The truth is, many people are only wolves in sheep's clothes. However, if we watch very closely, we will be able to see the true heart of the individuals we consider friends. If those we consider friends are dishonest, rude, have bad attitudes, and gossip, these are not people we should spend our time with. Paul says that these people influence us to create bad habits in our own lives. We should not keep company with such people. We should fellowship with Godly friends, those who help encourage us to grow in the character of Christ. Friends that speak truth in love, have wisdom, are encouraging, defend you, empathize, trusting, giving, confident, happy, selfless, peaceful, quiet spirits, non-judgmental, truthful, kind, consistent, and hopeful. Keeping this kind of company encourages good habits.

Lord, surround me with friends that encourage good habits and do not corrupt.

EXCELLENCE NOT MEDIOCRITY
"But earnestly desire the best gifts. And yet I show you a more excellent way."

1 Corinthians 12:31

My parents were great advocates of operating in excellence, especially when it came to the things of God. They held the same belief as Gordon B. Hinckley, "Mediocrity will never do. You are capable of something better." Good is the enemy of great, especially in the lives of Christians. We can get so comfortable with just being saved that we never grow in greater grace and knowledge of Jesus Christ. As Christians, we should never settle for doing things in a "good" way. Whatever we do, we should do out of a spirit of excellence. The desire for excellence is born out of love. Therefore, if love is our guiding principle, then everything we do will be covered in love. Mediocrity is unacceptable in the life of a Christian. Since God gave us his best, we should always strive to give him our best. This is the more excellent way.

Lord, lead me to always do everything with a sense of excellence and a spirit of love which is the more excellent way.

March 28
GLIMPSE OF GRACE

"When he came and had seen the grace of God, he was glad, and encouraged them all that with purpose of heart they should continue with the Lord."

Acts 11:23

My husband is an early riser. He usually wakes up between 4:45 and 5 AM every day. I follow (out of necessity) during the week between 5:15 and 5:30 AM. Which gives me time to hit the snooze button and get in some devotion. One time, my alarm failed to go off on a weekday! I had finally awakened and peeked at the clock on the nightstand. To my dismay, it read 5:58 AM! I was supposed to be leaving for work in 32 minutes! Amazingly, I got ready and still arrived at work earlier than usual. What I had received was a glimpse of grace. I didn't deserve to arrive early because I was guilty of oversleeping—but God! That is a glimpse of grace. We don't deserve the favor and goodness of the Lord, yet He gives it to us anyway.

Lord, let us always acknowledge when you provide us a glimpse of your grace.

March 29
DON'T GET WEARY

"And let us not grow weary while doing good, for in due season we shall reap if we do not lose heart..."

Galatians 6:9

I now understand why it has been said that ministry is a labor of love, emphasis on the word labor. God gives gifts to advance His kingdom. Therefore, you better believe that the more you operate in your gift, the more the enemy is going to try to attack. My gifts are those of the heart—encouragement(exhortation) and mercy. I continuously have people weighing on my heart and I try to minister to each one to the best of my ability. Sometimes my efforts are taken as judgmental even hypocritical! That has never been my intention. I only want what God wants for each of them and that is the best. (I have since learned that prayer is often the best thing I can do but that is another lesson, lol). The Lesson: Be not weary in well-doing.

Lord, thank you for the gifts you have given me. Let me use them to the best of my ability not to turn others away on offense, but to draw them closer to you by your love.

March 30
I'M PREY UNTIL I PRAY

"Be alert and of sober mind. Your enemy the devil prowls around like a roaring lion looking for someone to devour."

1 Peter 5:8

Prey can be defined as a person or thing easily injured or taken advantage of; victim, target. This is exactly what the enemy wants us to do to us. He wants us to become his prey. When we become prey, we have not heeded the warnings of the Word. The Bible tells us to be alert, that is watchful. To be sober-minded, keep the mind of Christ. We are to be watchful for the attacks of the enemy. When we fail to be alert, watchful, and sober-minded, we make ourselves prey. What we need to do is not be prey, but to pray. Prayer defeats the enemy by leading us into submission, which will allow us to resist him and he will flee. I am prey until I pray.

Lord, keep me in a prayerful mindset so that I will not fall prey to the enemy.

March 31
GOD PROVIDES

"And Abraham called the name of the place, The-Lord-Will-Provide; as it is said to this day, 'In the Mount of the Lord it shall be provided.'"

Genesis 22:14

One of the most hopeful promises of the Bible is the promise that God will provide. Throughout the Bible we are reminded over and over that whatever we need, God will supply. Philippians 4:19 reminds us that God will supply all of our needs according to His riches in glory by Christ Jesus. We can take comfort in knowing that God knows what we need, and He will be certain to supply it. We must trust that God knows what we need, when we need it. He will not fail to provide for his children! In trusting God to provide, we must also trust the timing of his provision! Though His timing may not always be comfortable, it is always perfect.

Lord, let me never forget that you will provide everything we need, when we need it because you are our provider.

APRIL

April 1
BLESSED IN STRANGE PLACES

"Then Isaac sowed in that land, and reaped in the same year a hundredfold; and the Lord blessed him."

Genesis 26:12

Our God specializes in things impossible! He can do the amazing, including blessing us in strange places. Has God ever blessed you in a strange place? God blessed Isaac in a strange place. Isaac sowed in a land of famine, a place of lack. But the blessing is that not only did Isaac sow in a place of famine, but the Lord blessed him in the midst of it. Not only did God bless him, but He also blessed him a hundredfold. Did you catch that? God blessed Isaac a hundredfold in the midst of famine! What about us? He will do the same for us. God will bless us in strange places if we follow his directions. If we stay in our famished places, God will bless us anyhow! He is just that kind of God who will bless us in strange places.

Lord, constantly remind me that you specialize in blessing us in strange places.

April 2

CONFIDENT NOT CONCEITED

"For the Lord will be your confidence, And will keep your foot from being caught."

Proverbs 3:26

As children of God, we can be confident that God has our back! Sometimes, being in His will results in us doing things that the world may not necessarily believe! Being in His will sometimes pushes us to make faith moves that don't make sense to those around us. It can sometimes be difficult to be immovable in God's direction, especially when we don't receive the "yes" or the confirmation of man. Today, I want to encourage you to be confident in the will of God. Rest assured that He will not cause you to slip up or fall on your face. Remember, His plan is for you to become prosperous. He has designed an amazing future for you. When others shake their heads at you in disbelief, hold your head high and stay in the will of God. Remember that your confidence doesn't come from their validation. Instead, your confidence comes from knowing that God won't leave you or forsake you!

Lord, let my confidence continue to be in you.

April 3
MEANT FOR GOOD

"But as for you, you meant evil against me; but God meant it for good, in order to bring it about as it is this day, to save many people alive."

Genesis 50:20

So many times in our lives, it seems that situations will not work out for our good. However, they always work out for good. As Christians, we should not be surprised but rather walk in confidence knowing that God has promised that all things work together for good. Unfortunately, we have taken these verses to mean that things will always work for our good. However, closer examination shows that the Bible tells us that things will always work together for good. It may be for our good or the good of others. But we can rest assured that it will work out for good. What the enemy meant to destroy us, distract us, and discourage us, God meant it for good.

Lord, whenever the devil means me harm work all things out for good.

April 4
DO THE RIGHT THING

"And so it was, because the midwives feared God, that He provided households for them."

Exodus 1:21

Integrity should be a mark of Christian character. Integrity is doing the right thing, whether someone is watching or not, whether someone knows you did it or not. Integrity is doing it simply because it is the right thing to do. This is exactly what the midwives did. They stood in integrity because they feared God. With Christ in our lives, we are empowered to do the right thing. Check out these quotes about integrity:

"Real integrity" is doing the right thing, knowing that nobody's going to know whether you did it or not."

— Oprah Winfrey

"If it is not right do not do it; if it is not true do not say it."

— Marcus Aurelius

"Every man must decide whether he will walk in the light of creative altruism or in the darkness of destructive selfishness."

— Martin Luther King Jr.

"Integrity is doing the right thing, even if nobody is watching."

— Jim Stovall

Lord, strengthen me to live a life of integrity.

April 5
TRUST ISSUES

"God is not a man, that He should lie, nor a son of man, that He should repent. Has He said, and will He not do? Or has He spoken, and will He not make it good?"

Numbers 23:19

The Bible is full of the promises of God if we would only take time to read them. The beauty of the promises of God is that they are certain, they are true, and they will come to past. In Numbers, God reminds us that He is not a man. He doesn't lie. What He has said He will do. We can rest assured that He can do everything that He has said He would do. Sometimes, it can be hard for us to trust God because of the many times we've had our hearts broken by other people. Understand that as human beings, we are not perfect. However, we serve a perfect God who won't ever fail us! If God made you a promise, you can rest assured that He will see to It! Every Word that comes from His mouth accomplishes that in which He set it out to accomplish. God's Words never return to Him void.

Lord, let me always remember that you will do just what you said.

April 6
WHEN GOD SAYS MOVE

"See, I have set the land before you; go in and possess the land..."

Deuteronomy 1:8a

We will follow the instructions of everyone but God. We ask Iyanla Vandzant to fix our lives. We do everything that Oprah does or says. We follow every suggestion of Dr. Oz as well as Dr. Phil. But when it comes to the things of God, we are hesitant to follow and obey. God has provided specific guidance for life in His Word. The Bible guides us in the ways He would have us to go. Even when we can't see the complete path before us, we can be confident in taking steps with God. Today, condition your mind and heart to submit to the directions of God as easily as you submit to the suggestions of others. From this day forward, allow God's instructions to be your guiding light!

Lord, when you say move, I will move.

April 7
TRAIN UP A CHILD

"Train up a child in the way he should go, and when he is old he will not depart from it."

Proverbs 22:6

Men of Honor is one of my favorite movies. In the movie, MASNF is inscribed on the homemade radio made by the father of Carl Brashear. The acronym stands for "A Son Never Forgets." It means a child never forgets the sacrifice others have made on their behalf in order for them to follow their dream. Never forget where you come from. Never forget how you were raised. If we train up our children and the children under our influence in the love and admonition of the Lord, they will retain it. They will keep that upbringing with them the rest of their lives. I am a witness! I was raised by two parents who loved and served the Lord, and they passed that love of the Lord on to me. Even if you do not have children of your own, be sure to be a living example of God's love in the presence of those in your sphere of influence.

Lord, when I am weary or in despair let me look back at the lessons of childhood and the legacy my parents left me in you.

April 8
MENTORING MATTERS
"Mentoring is sharing life's experiences and God's faithfulness"
Janet Thompson

Mentoring is essential to Christians. Both to be mentored and to mentor. Many Christians of all ages desire to be mentored and to mentor themselves. Chronological age is not as important as spiritual age. A mentor is someone who shares life experiences and God's faithfulness. That is as simple as it is complex. It is the job of both mentors and mentees to encourage and strengthen. We should all have persons who mentor us professionally, personally, and of course spiritually. Also, we should prayerfully seek people to mentor professionally, personally, and spiritually.

Lord, let me find mentors professionally, personally, and spiritually and let me be a mentor as well.

April 9

COMING OUT FROM HIDING

"Now when the woman saw that she was not hidden, she came trembling; and falling down before Him, she declared to Him in the presence of all the people the reason she had touched Him and how she was healed immediately."

Luke 8:47

The woman in this scripture had been dealing with internal issues that caused her to be shunned by everyone in town. As a result, she hid herself. When Jesus came in to town, however, she stepped out amongst everyone, touched His hem, and was healed. Jesus said, "Someone touched me!" (paraphrasing) The woman realized that she could no longer hide and came forth. When she admitted to touching Jesus, Jesus told her that because of her faith, she had been healed. Her healing came as a result of her stepping out, despite how people had rejected her, and seeking the help of the one she knew could make her whole.

Some of us have been wearing masks for much of our lives. We have hidden our brokenness behind masks of happiness. We have pridefully hidden our financial struggles behind lavish lifestyles. We have hidden our heartbreak behind new relationships. What we must realize is that our healing can only come through our openness and honesty. God has intentionally placed people in our paths who can help us. What we must do is remove the mask, be honest about our struggles, and allow those God has placed in our path to love us to a place of wholeness.

Lord, let me know that I can take off my mask in your presence and when I do so I will no longer need it again.

April 10
I AM WHAT I AM

"But by the grace of God I am what I am, and His grace toward me was not in vain;"
1 Corinthians 5:10 (NKJV)

"But by God's grace I am what I am, and His grace toward me was not ineffective."
1 Corinthians 5:10 (HCSB)

"But because God was so gracious, so very generous, here I am. And I'm not about to let his grace go to waste."
1 Corinthians 5:10 (MSG)

I asked my prayer friends who they were before Christ came into their lives. They replied incomplete, lost, confused, gullible, vulnerable, selfish, broken, self-focused, self-reliant, proud, and self-righteous. Then I asked them who they were now that Christ has come into their lives. They replied: redeemed, saved, blessed, highly favored, forgiven, changed...

We are who we are only because of the grace of God. If it wasn't for the grace of God, where would we be? We may not be all that we should be. However, we can praise God that we are not what we used to be!

Lord, thank you for your unmerited favor toward us that was gracious and generous.

April 11
THE BEST IS YET TO COME

"The end of a thing is better than its beginning; The patient in spirit is better than the proud in spirit."

Ecclesiastes 7:8

I praise Your Name, God! Lord, you are so loving towards us and good to us, even though we don't deserve it. You continue to work in our lives in such a way that we know it's the Lord's doing and it's marvelous in our eyes. You have healed us, healed our loved ones, you have watched over our children and our families, provided all our needs according to your riches-our jobs, food on the table, transportation. You name it! You have broken chains, lifted bowed down heads, and done exceedingly abundantly above and beyond all that we ask or think or imagine! Thank you! We are not perfect, but because of your grace we are better than we were. Thank you for breaking the bonds of sin that so easily beset us. Lord, whatever or whoever is hindering our walk with you, remove from our presence. Forgive us for every sin and lead us in right paths. Lord, whatever you're doing in this season, don't do it without us. Remind us daily that you are bigger than anything we are facing. You're bigger than the President, our supervisors, our titles...you are BIGGER! Lord, thank you for the confidence we have in you that if we ask anything in your will, you will do it. We praise you in advance, knowing that you will provide!

Lord, always lead me to pray—praise, repent, ask, and yield.

April 12
PRAY UNTIL SOMETHING HAPPENS

"Pray in the Spirit at all times and on every occasion. Stay alert and be persistent in your prayers for all believers everywhere."

Ephesians 6:18

We need to be more careful when we purpose to be more prayerful. God will hear and answer. We may not always like the answer either. The current political climate is forcing me to stand on God's word of loving those who don't love God or us for that matter. I had to daily pray for strength to love people I quite frankly don't like. God spoke to my spirit during devotion that I'm hindering my prayers when I am not honest about my true feelings or intents toward others. When we continue to practice the very sin, we should be putting away, or worse when we justify the sin we're in. But if we continue to ignore the sin glaring us in the face each day, it is all vanity. And self-righteousness. And hypocrisy. And a stumbling block. Transparency is never easy, but it is necessary. We want our prayers to be heard, and we want them answered. I was therefore prompted to see if there was anything else that could be hindering my prayers, crippling my prayer life, or causing other prayer friends to stumble. I don't know about you, but there is too much going on in my life and the lives of those around me for me to allow my prayers to be hindered by anything.

Lord forgive me and I ask that you forgive any sin that may have hindered my prayers.

April 13
I CAN'T HEAR YOU

"But your iniquities have separated you from your God; your sins have hidden his face from you, so that he will not hear."

Isaiah 59:2 (NIV)

One thing is for sure, we are far from perfect. The beautiful thing is, God knows we are not perfect. Before Jesus Christ died for the atonement of our sins, people had to make sacrifices and have priests to atone for their sins. The blood of Jesus gives us the freedom to go before God and repent for our sins. When we repent with our hearts, He will forgive our sins.

Because we are human beings, we may not always be quickly aware of the sins we commit. For this reason, we must make sure that whenever we pray, we repent for the things we did knowingly and unknowingly. We must make it a habit to repent before we ask God for anything. Today, remember to repent for any wrongs you have committed. Know in your heart that your heavenly Father has forgiven you.

Lord, I am confessing. I am repenting. I don't want to be repeating. Forgive me.

April 14

MY SISTER/BROTHER'S KEEPER

"Make this your common practice: confess your sins to each other and pray for each other so that you can live together whole and healed."

James 5:16a (MSG)

As Christians, we should take time each day to intercede on behalf of our sisters and brothers. We each face so much on a daily basis. If we want to be healed and we want to be whole, we need to confess to our accountability partners and pray diligently and intentionally. In fact, the Bible says that we should make confession and pray for one another daily. Think about your circle of friends. What are their needs? How could you pray for them today? Consider your circle, name by name and need by need. Each day during your devotion or whenever you are led by the Spirit, pray for all the needs of your sisters and brothers. Pray because we are instructed to do so in God's word. Pray because our sisters and brothers need prayer. Pray because we are our sister/brother's keeper.

Lord, I will confess my sins to my accountability partner, and I will pray diligently, sincerely, and intercede on behalf of my circle.

April 15
MADE BY THE MASTER

"For you created my inmost being; you knit me together in my mother's womb. I praise you because I am fearfully and wonderfully made; your works are wonderful, I know that full well."

Psalm 139:14 (NIV)

We are God's special creation. As Christians, we must strive to live lives holy and acceptable unto God. The enemy is constantly trying to hinder our prayers, discourage us, and stir up distrust and strife. Why? Because the prayers of the righteous are powerful and effective! We must remember who we are. Unfortunately, anything that God wants to do, Satan is opposed. And he seeks to get us to do, be, or have anything God has not called us to do, be, or have. Then, what happens? It stirs up doubt and strife. Maybe we aren't getting that new boo, new job, or new promotion, etc. because God hasn't ordained for us to have them. Maybe, just maybe, God has something different and far greater prepared for us!

Lord, constantly remind us that there is nothing wrong with us, we were fearfully and wonderfully made by you.

April 16
UNDESERVED

"For it is by grace you have been saved, through faith—
and this is not from yourselves, it is the gift of God—
not by works, so that no one can boast."

Ephesians 2:8-9 (NIV)

Have you ever really considered the significance of grace? Grace is getting what we do not deserve. Grace is God saying yes, when he could have said no. Grace is unmerited favor. Grace is the core of the Bible. Grace is God's love when we don't want or deserve it. Grace is free, but not cheap. Grace is God's Riches At Christ's Expense. Grace is a gift.

Think about it...He has woken us up to brand new days, even when we have sinned against Him before we fell asleep. He has blessed us with what we need even after we squandered away His blessings on the things that we wanted. God has kept us safe when we have knowingly placed ourselves in the path of danger. God's grace for us in unexplainable. It cannot be earned by good deeds. It is a gift from God given to us when we didn't even know we needed it. Today, take some time and thank God for His Grace! Thank Him for always giving you what you need, but never what you deserved!

Lord, you are a loving and wonderful God! Your grace said yes. Thank you, Lord!

April 17
UNFAIR FIGHT

"The Lord will fight for you; you need only to be still."

Exodus 14:14 (NIV)

Fighting on our knees is what Christians do best. Well, it is what Christians *should* do best. Unfortunately, fighting on our knees is not always our first response...or second. It is often our last resort. God has promised us that He will fight for us, all we have to do is be still. It is there in that the problem lies. Sometimes, we fail to be still and allow the Lord to fight for us. The Bible tells us in Psalm 46:10 (NIV), "Be still, and know that I am God;" and in Psalm 37:7 (NIV), "Be still before the Lord and wait patiently for him; do not fret when people succeed in their ways, when they carry out their wicked schemes." If only we would be still, let go, and let God. He will fight for us. It will be an unfair fight, and we will win.

Lord, help me to be still and let you fight for me.

April 18
MARVELOUS

"This was the Lord's doing; It is marvelous in our eyes."
Psalm 118:23

Have you ever thought about the marvelous things that God has done in our lives? Everything God has done in our lives is marvelous. Though we have endured some difficult times, God has done some pretty amazing things in our lives! During the times when it feels like everything is going wrong, we have to take a moment and think back on the amazing things God has already done for us. Sometimes, we take for granted the "small things" God does for us like waking us up in the morning, keeping us in our right minds, protecting our family and love ones, and loving us enough to provide the things we need! The next time you are feeling down about something you don't have, take a moment and think about the marvelous things God has done on your behalf!

Lord, everything you do is marvelous in our eyes!

April 19
WHAT HAD HAPPENED

"And he took him by the right hand and lifted him up, and immediately his feet and ankle bones received strength. So he, leaping up, stood and walked and entered the temple with them—walking, leaping, and praising God. And all the people saw him walking and praising God. Then they knew that it was he who sat begging alms at the Beautiful Gate of the temple; and they were filled with wonder and amazement at what had happened to him."

Acts 3:7-10

Andrae Crouch summarized the salvation experience in his lyrics: "*Somebody told me of the joy they had. And somebody told me that in sorrow they could be glad. Then they told me once they were bound but now set free. But I didn't think it could be until it happened to me. But now I can tell you of the joy I have. And now I can tell you that in sorrow I can be glad. And now I can tell you once I was bound but now set free. But you'll never know that it's true until it happens to you.*" The transformation of salvation is amazing. When people ask me to describe the experience, I am completely speechless! I don't know how to explain it or describe it. Have you ever felt like this? Today, take some time and think about your salvation. Take it a step further and even attempt to journal how it feels!

Lord, I wouldn't know this could be until it happened to me.

April 20
BE CAREFUL LITTLE MOUTH

"Don't tear down another person with your words. Instead, keep the peace, and be considerate. Be truly humble toward everyone."

Titus 3:2 (VOICE)

My elementary teacher was wrong. Words do hurt. Lies and gossip have destroyed many relationships. Half-truths and lies have done a lot of damage. Titus warns us to speak evil of no one. Instead, we should strive to keep the peace and be considerate. We should be truly humble toward everyone. Today, make it your goal to only speak positively of everyone around you. From the president to your boss, make it your business to not let any evil words come from your mouth about anyone.

Lord, let me be mindful of the words that I speak to and about others.

April 21
YOU CAN BE HEALED

"Now a woman, having a flow of blood for twelve years, who had spent all her livelihood on physicians and could not be healed by any, came from behind and touched the border of His garment. And immediately her flow of blood stopped."

Luke 8:43-44

Can you imagine being ill for 12 years? I'm pretty sure that woman began to feel like she was hopeless. I'm pretty sure that those around her may have made her feel like her condition was hopeless. Maybe you've never been physically ill, so you can't relate, but I'm pretty sure that you've experienced some type of heartache from a broken relationship, losing someone close to you, or even a bad break-up. In our time of despair, it can feel like we are doomed to be in pain forever. This is not so. God can and will heal our minds, bodies, and hearts. In order to receive his healing, we must have faith and believe in our hearts that we can be healed. We have to trust that God can cause us to become whole. Today, I want you to take your infirmity to God. It can be an infirmity of your heart, mind, or body. Take it to God and have faith that He can heal you. The Bible tells us that by the stripes Jesus took for us, we are healed. It is not God's plan for us to be ill. We have to put a demand on God's healing power and believe with everything in us that He can heal us.

Lord, thank you in advance for healing me!

April 22

LOVE IS WHAT LOVE DOES

"Love is patient, love is kind. It does not envy, it does not boast, it is not proud. It does not dishonor others, it is not self-seeking, it is not easily angered, it keeps no record of wrongs. Love does not delight in evil but rejoices with the truth. It always protects, always trusts, always hopes, always perseveres. Love never fails."
1 Corinthians 13:4-8a (NIV)

There is an anonymous quote that says, "I asked Jesus, 'how much do you love me?' 'This much' he replied. Then He stretched out his arms and died." The Bible is very clear about love. Especially God's love for us. The clearest definition of love can be found in the "love" chapter of the Bible 1 Corinthians 13. It tells us what love is, but more than that it tells us what love does. Love is an action word. Love is what love does....Our goal should be to live in a way that exudes the love of God. Yes, we will encounter people who we feel do not deserve our love, but remember, Jesus Christ died for them too! If He loves them that much, then so should you. Let you LOVE shine bright today.

Lord, you are a loving and wonderful God, and you have shown us what love is.

April 23
IT'S ALL GOOD

"And we know [with great confidence] that God [who is deeply concerned about us] causes all things to work together [as a plan] for good for those who love God, to those who are called according to His plan and purpose."

Romans 8:28 (AMP)

Romans 8:28 is one of the most misquoted scriptures in the Bible. We often hear people say, "We know that God works all things together for our good." Careful examination of the passage reveals that things are not worked together for our good, but for good. Yes, it's all good, but it's all God, and sometimes God doesn't work things together for our own personal good but rather for the good of others. Everything isn't about us, but it is all God. So when it is all God, it is all good.

Lord, remind me daily that it is indeed all good because it is all God.

April 24
HONEY FROM THE ROCK

"He nourished him with honey from the rock,"

Deuteronomy 32:13b (NIV)

Life can be hard. Trials, troubles, and difficulties make it difficult. However, we serve a God that brings sweetness out of the hard places in life. In the hard places of life we should reflect on the many ways God can bring honey from the rock. Honey from the rock includes anxiety into assurance, burdens into blessings, fear into faith, and pain into praise. Our God satisfies us with honey from the rock, bringing sweetness out of the hard places of life.

Lord, thank you for bringing sweetness out of the hard places of life.

April 25
LEANING ON THE EVERLASTING ARMS

"The eternal God is your refuge,
and underneath are the everlasting arms."

Deuteronomy 33:27a (NIV)

There are meanings and messages in the hymns we sing at church. One encouraging hymn is, *Leaning On the Everlasting Arms*. The second verse and refrain reflect the words of the Deuteronomy passage above. *"Leaning, leaning, safe and secure from all alarms; leaning, leaning, leaning on the everlasting arms. What have I to dread, what have I to fear, leaning on the everlasting arms? I have blessed peace with my Lord so near, leaning on the everlasting arms."* God is our refuge, and we find safety underneath His everlasting arms. There is no place as secure as in the everlasting arms. Someone once said that the safest place in the world is in the middle of the will of God.

Lord, you are my refuge, and I find safety and security underneath your everlasting arms.

April 26
GOD IS...

"God is with you in everything you do."

Genesis 21:22b

In *God Is* by James Cleveland, he says: God is my protection... my light in darkness...joy in time of sorrow...my today and tomorrow...the joy and the strength of my life...my all and all. One of my favorite phrases in the Bible is "God is..." Whatever we need, God is that. When we need reassurance, God confirms us. When we need help standing, we only need to be reminded that God is within us, so we will not fall. If we need to be fortified, God is our fortress. When we are uncertain, God is faithful. Whatever we need, God is. Not God was, or will be. Whatever we need, God is.

Lord, thank you for being whatever it is that I need.

April 27
WORTH-SHIP

"As she stood behind him at his feet weeping, she began to wet his feet with her tears. Then she wiped them with her hair, kissed them and poured perfume on them.."

Luke 7:38

The dictionary defines worship: show reverence and adoration for; honor with religious rites; revere, reverence, venerate, pay homage to, honor, adore, praise, pray to, glorify, exalt, extol; hold dear, cherish, treasure, esteem, adulate. For Christians, worship is where we show God his worth to us. Worship shows God His worth-ship to us. It is where we praise God for what He has done. Worship is for who God is. His redemptive power makes Him worthy of our worship. When we worship, we show God His worth to us.

Lord, you are worthy of our worship and deserve all the glory, honor, and adoration.

April 28
CAN'T GET RIGHT

"On a Sabbath Jesus was teaching in one of the synagogues, and a woman was there who had been crippled by a spirit for eighteen years. She was bent over and could not straighten up at all. When Jesus saw her, he called her forward and said to her, 'Woman, you are set free from your infirmity.'"

Luke 13:10-12 (NIV)

Our sin condition before we meet Christ is one where we "can't get right." We spend time trying to fix ourselves, and get ourselves right when all along we are unable to do so. The truth is we can't "get right" without God. We can't get right unless Jesus gets us right. As Christians, we sit in church service week after week bent over by life and unable to straighten ourselves up. Then comes Jesus, just like the woman in the Luke passage. There was a woman who had been bent over and could not straighten up for eighteen years. Then along came Jesus and He set her free. When Jesus comes into our lives, he straightens out the crooked places of our lives that we can't get right.

Lord, only you can straighten up our bent over and crooked lives.

April 29
RETURN TO SENDER

"What shall I return to the Lord for all his goodness to me? I will lift up the cup of salvation and call on the name of the Lord."
Psalm 116:12-13 (NIV)

O ne songwriter asked, *"How can I say thanks, for the things you have done for me? Things so undeserved, yet you do to prove your love for me. The voices of a million angels, could not express my gratitude. All that I am or ever hope to be, I owe it all to thee."* In these lyrics, the songwriter poses a very powerful question that the psalmist had asked centuries before. What can we possibly give back to God for all He has given to us? The psalmist advises us to lift up a drink offering unto the Lord. That is to offer libations or pour out in remembrance of Jesus pouring out His own blood on our behalf. Because of salvation, we also have the privilege of approaching God in prayer. We can call on his name. So the drink offering and prayer are what we return to God.

Lord, thank you for the gift of salvation. May I always pour unto you praise and prayer in return.

April 30
POSITIONED TO PRAY

"But when you pray, go away by yourself, shut the door behind you, and pray to your Father in private. Then your Father, who sees everything, will reward you. "When you pray, don't babble on and on as the Gentiles do. They think their prayers are answered merely by repeating their words again and again. Don't be like them, for your Father knows exactly what you need even before you ask him!"

Matthew 6: 6-8 (NLT)

The right position to pray is based on the posture of your heart, not the posture of your body. Whether you choose to kneel, bow, stand, or lie prostrate, if your heart is not in the right position to pray your body is irrelevant. Your heart should be positioned to praise; give God the praise that he is due. It should be positioned to repent; ask God to forgive any sin that will hinder our requests. It should be positioned to ask; the scripture reminds us that God already knows what we need before we ask. Finally, it should be positioned to yield; submit fully to the will of God. Then we are properly positioned to pray.

Lord, position us to pray. Bow our hearts and humble our minds before you.

MAY

May 1
FIRST THINGS FIRST

"Seek the Kingdom of God above all else, and live righteously, and he will give you everything you need."

Matthew 6: 33 (NLT)

God will supply everything we need if we seek the Kingdom of God above all else and live right. Seeking the Kingdom of God is to seek God and the things of God. To do that, we must make sure that our intentions are correct. We must ensure that we are in love with the Creator and not his creations. We must love the Giver and not gifts. When our hearts are focused on loving God, we can live right. Living right is a reflection of our love of God. It is His love that empowers us to walk right, talk right, and live right. If we do these two things: seek God first and live right, then we will have everything we need. Put first things first.

Lord, help me put you first and live right.

May 2
ROTTEN FRUIT

"You can identify them by their fruit, that is, by the way they act."
Galatians 5:19-21 (CEV)

The Bible tells us that a tree cannot bear both good and bad fruit. We are identified by the fruit we bear. Bad fruit is works of the flesh. They include immoral ways, filthy thoughts, shameful deeds, idolatry, witchcraft, hatred, and confusion. If these things are evident in our lives, then we are bearing bad fruit. The fruit of the Spirit should be prevalent in our lives. The fruit of the spirit are love, joy, self-control, kindness, peace, patience, goodness, gentleness, and faithfulness. We should be known by these fruit. People should be able to recognize that we are children of the most high because of these fruit! When we bear these fruit, we don't have to shout our love from God from the rooftops. Instead, it will be evident in the way we live.

Lord, help me to bear good fruit and not rotten fruit.

May 3
BE ATTITUDES

"Blessed are the poor in spirit, For theirs is the kingdom of heaven. Blessed are those who mourn, For they shall be comforted. Blessed are the meek, For they shall inherit the earth. Blessed are those who hunger and thirst for righteousness, For they shall be filled. Blessed are the merciful, For they shall obtain mercy. Blessed are the pure in heart, For they shall see God. Blessed are the peacemakers, For they shall be called sons of God. Blessed are those who are persecuted for righteousness' sake, For theirs is the kingdom of heaven."

Matthew 5:3-10

According to Roy T. Bennett, "Attitude is a choice. Happiness is a choice. Optimism is a choice. Kindness is a choice. Giving is a choice. Respect is a choice. Whatever choice you make makes you. Choose wisely." The Bible instructs us on how our attitudes should be. We should have attitudes that are dependent on God, humble, obedient, merciful, pure hearts, and peaceful. Our attitudes are so important. Our attitudes determine our altitude. Our attitudes determine our being. Most of all we should have the attitude of Christ. Many times, we refrain from having the attitude of Christ because of things that others have done to us. We must realize that sometimes, all it takes for someone to change is one encounter with God. Nine times out of ten, the unsaved individuals we encounter don't go to church. However, an encounter with a true Christian who has the attitude of Christ can lead them to salvation. In your day to day interactions, strive to radiate the attitude of Christ. You never know who your life may be ministering to!

Lord, let me always have an attitude of gratitude.

May 4

LOVER NOT A HATER

"You have heard that it was said, 'Love your neighbor and hate your enemy.' But I tell you, love your enemies and pray for those who persecute you, that you may be children of your Father in heaven. He causes his sun to rise on the evil and the good, and sends rain on the righteous and the unrighteous. If you love those who love you, what reward will you get?"

Matthew 5:43-46a

The Urban Dictionary defines a hater as a person who simply cannot be happy for another person's success. So rather than be happy, they make a point of exposing a flaw in that person. Hating is not exactly jealousy. The hater doesn't want to be the person he or she hates; rather the hater wants to knock someone else down a notch. In this world, haters are going to hate. It is not uncommon for us to experience haters, however, as children of God, we are called to love. Even though someone may intentionally try to tear us down, we must not respond in the same hatred that has been shown to us. At all times, we must choose to respond in love. Yes, I know it may be difficult from time to time. Trust that your heavenly Father sees everything and will reward your effort to live in His image.

Lord, help me to have a heart of love.

May 5

YES WE CAN

"I can do all things [which He has called me to do] through Him who strengthens and empowers me [to fulfill His purpose—I am self-sufficient in Christ's sufficiency; I am ready for anything and equal to anything through Him who infuses me with inner strength and confident peace."
Philippians 4:13 (AMP)

One of the most memorable speeches that President Barak Obama gave was during the New Hampshire primary. The speech is most often referred to as the "Yes, We Can" speech. It reminds us of the American spirit. One line in particular says, "For when we have faced down impossible odds, when we've been told we're not ready or that we shouldn't try or that we can't, generations of Americans have responded with a simple creed that sums up the spirit of people; Yes we can. Yes, we can. Yes, we can." Even though President Obama inspired us with his words, the original "Yes We Can" speech was written in the book of Philippians. There we find the promise that we can do everything through Christ who strengthens us. It is our Lord and Savior that gives us the strength to do whatever He has for us to do.

Lord, I can do all things through you.

May 6
GET INFORMATION

"Get wisdom, get understanding; do not forget my words or turn away from them."

Proverbs 4:5 (NIV)

Beyoncé released "Formation" in 2016 and encouraged ladies to get "in formation." Likewise, Christians need to get "information" from the Word of God aka wisdom. Now there is a difference in knowledge and wisdom. Knowledge is facts, information, and skills acquired by a person through experience or education. Wisdom is the quality of having experience, knowledge, and good judgment or the quality of being wise. The world encourages us to gain knowledge and to accumulate a lot of useless information. But wisdom is from above. Wisdom is covered the truth of God's word. The only way to get wisdom is to ask God for it and get it from His Word. Not only will God give it to us, but God will also give it to us liberally.

Lord, grant us your information and wisdom from above.

May 7
RICH DAD

"And my God shall supply all your need according to His riches in glory by Christ Jesus."

Philippians 4:19 (NKJV)

Do you have any idea how rich our heavenly father is? Everything on this Earth belongs to Him! The Bible even tells us that the heart of the king lies in His hands. I don't know about you, but this gives me assurance that there is nothing I need that is out of His reach. The Bible also tells us that He will withhold no good thing from us. This lets us know that when we have needs, we can present them to God and He will take care of us. Many of us worry because our provision doesn't always come in the way we expect it. Sometimes, we expect grand miracles and overlook the simplicity of God's provision. Some of us would rather wait for a unexpected check in the mail than to accept help from the loving friends and family God has surrounded us with. Nothing is wrong with expecting God to do the impossible, but we must be careful not to overlook or be unappreciative of the way He desires to bless us. If He blesses others to be a blessing to you, put your pride to the side and accept it.

Today, remind yourself that God can provide every one of your needs. Everything belongs to our Daddy and there is nothing we need that won't be provided to us in His perfect timing.

Lord, thank you for providing my needs. Help me to be open to the many ways you choose to provide for me!

May 8
ACT BRAND NEW

"Therefore, if anyone is in Christ, he is a new creation; old things have passed away; behold, all things have become new."

2 Corinthians 5:17 (NKJV)

The Urban Dictionary defines "brand new" as "acting a certain way or displaying characteristics that are not congruent with one's normal behavior." Although in secular culture this is viewed negatively, realistically we should all act brand new. If we are in Christ, we are "brand new." We become a new creation. Our old ways pass away and we should display characteristics that are not what people are used to seeing in us. All things become new. If we have been born again, we should all be acting "brand new."

Lord, thank you for being a loving and wonderful God who makes me brand new through salvation.

May 9

INSIDE OUT

"Brothers and sisters, in light of all I have shared with you about God's mercies, I urge you to offer your bodies as a living and holy sacrifice to God, a sacred offering that brings Him pleasure; this is your reasonable, essential worship. Do not allow this world to mold you in its own image. Instead, be transformed from the inside out by renewing your mind. As a result, you will be able to discern what God wills and whatever God finds good, pleasing, and complete."

Romans 12:1-2 (VOICE)

The Bible tells us to offer our bodies as a living and holy sacrifice unto God. The problem with a living sacrifice is that it can get up off the altar at any time and walk away. Unfortunately, we often do. Outside pressures can move us to stop living holy and go back to our unholy ways. The least we can do is make sure our actions are pleasing to God. We cannot be intimidated when the world calls us out as "holy, holy" and they will. We cannot allow our image to conform to the world. Constantly transforming our mind to the mind of Christ allows us to discern the will of God. That is what changes us from the inside out.

Lord, make me a living sacrifice that holy and acceptable unto you.

May 10

BECAUSE I CAN, DOESN'T MEAN I SHOULD

"I have the right to do anything," you say—but not everything is beneficial."

1 Corinthians 6:12a (NIV)

Freedom in Christ means that we are free to do what we want to do. Although we can do anything, everything is not beneficial. Our words and deeds should be covered by the Word of God. While some things are not good, there are some things that we should not do merely because of their appearance. As a Christians, we should model Christ with our lips and lives. Some things are not necessarily sin, but if they would cause someone else to stumble in their walk with Christ, we should not do or say them. God has given us free will so that we can freely choose to love and follow Him, not the world.

Lord, let everything I do or say bring you glory or edify other people.

May 11
PRICELESS

" You are not your own; you were bought at a price. Therefore honor God with your bodies."

1 Corinthians 6:20 (NIV)

On September 10, 1776, General George Washington asked for a volunteer for a hazardous mission: to gather intelligence behind enemy lines before the coming Battle of Harlem Heights. Captain Nathan Hale of the 19th Regiment of the Continental Army stepped forward and subsequently become one of the first known American spies of the Revolutionary War. Disguised as a Dutch schoolmaster, the Yale University-educated Hale slipped behind British lines on Long Island and successfully gathered information about British troop movements for the next several weeks. On September 21, 1776, Hale was captured while sailing Long Island Sound, trying to cross back into an American-controlled territory. Hale was interrogated by British General William Howe. When it was discovered that he was carrying incriminating documents, General Howe ordered his execution for spying, which was set for the following morning. After being led to the gallows, legend holds that Hale was asked if he had any last words and he replied with the now-famous words, "I only regret that I have but one life to give for my country." At the age of 21, Nathan Hale was hanged by the British on the morning of September 22, 1776. We, like Hale, have only one life to live for the Lord. It is a priceless gift that we should handle with care. One of my older relatives proclaims each family reunion that, if she lives, she will live for Christ and if she dies, she will live with Christ. Life with Christ—priceless.

Lord, your gift of salvation is priceless, let me always treat it as such.

May 12
KNOW THAT YOU KNOW

"Study to shew thyself approved unto God, a workman that
needeth not to be ashamed, rightly dividing the word of truth."
2 Timothy 2:15(KJV)

We say and believe so many things that are not in the Bible. Over the years, people have taken certain things from the Bible and gotten the wrong interpretation or created an interpretation that best fits their situation. As a result, these interpretations travel, and many mistakenly take them to be true.

As Christians, it is essential that we know the Word of God. Otherwise, we will believe things that aren't in His word. More so, we will repeat and encourage others with words that are not from God's word. Below are three things I've often heard that are not in the Bible. Beside each of them, you will find the appropriate scripture. Read the scriptures and ask God to give you the correct interpretation. Be sure to erase these incorrect sayings from your mind, and replace them with the rightly divided word of Truth!

1. God will never give you more than you can bear. (1 Corinthians 10:13)
2. God works in mysterious ways. (Romans 11:33)
3. Money is the root of all evil. (Timothy 6:10)

We have to know the word of God for ourselves. The only way to know the truth is to study. Then, you know that you *know* what you know.

Lord, guide me in learning and studying your Word.

May 13

EXAMINE, TEST, AND KNOW

"Examine yourselves as to whether you are in the faith. Test yourselves. Do you not know yourselves, that Jesus Christ is in you?—unless indeed you are disqualified."

2 Corinthians 13:5

I f we want to evaluate our relationship with Christ, it is important that we take time to examine ourselves, test ourselves, and then know ourselves... First, we should examine ourselves honestly. Our accountability partners can assist us in this area. Have I been walking in faith? Then we are to test ourselves. Is Christ in us? Finally, we need to know ourselves. We know when we are walking by faith and when we are walking by sight. We know when we are walking by faith and when we are walking in our flesh. The more we get into God's word, the more easily we will be able to examine ourselves, test ourselves, and know ourselves.

Lord, quicken my spirit so that I will examine myself, test myself, and know myself.

May 14
PRAYER PARTNERS

"For where two or three gather in my name, there am I with them."

Matthew 18:20 (NIV)

According to Karen Scalf Linamen in her book *Parent Warrior*, there are benefits of praying together: "It makes you accountable." On our own, we get distracted by the demands of life. Knowing that we have scheduled prayer times helps us budget our time and focus on prayer. "It develops intimacy." There are so few chances for an intimate connection with others. We long to connect with others in a significant way. Prayer with others cuts to the soul and allows sharing of struggles, disappointments, hopes, and blessings. "It offers a time to express the power of God's unconditional love and acceptance." There is healing when we share our deepest secret with a prayer partner - and that partner still loves us. When that happens, it's easier to believe that God, whom we can't see, can love us that way too - and more. "It gives us the opportunity to experience God's love in a physical, tangible manner." It makes God's love real - a place to give hugs, pats on the back, and for holding hands and wiping tears. When Prayer Partners are around, God is definitely in the midst.

Lord, thank you for iron sharpening, encouraging prayer partners.

May 15
FROM RAGGEDY TO RIGHTEOUS

"Let all things be done decently and in order."

1 Corinthians 14:40

There should be a clear distinction between our conduct before Christ came into our lives and after. The definition of decent is "conforming with generally accepted standards of respectable or moral behavior." The definition of raggedy is scruffy or shabby. Reality TV provides us clear distinctions between the two behaviors. Unfortunately, modern "reality" shows provide some of the best (worst) examples of raggedy behavior. Perhaps unreal TV is a better description of the programming. Christ should be seen in our conduct, whether we are babes in Christ or seasoned saints. Before Christ, we were raggedy, but now as Christians, our lives are righteous. We must be careful not to conform to the world's standards of living. Despite the impression certain television shows may place upon us, we must remember that as Christians, the God life is our only way of life. Anything that opposes how God has instructed us to live is raggedy. Though the pressure may be hard at times, we should always strive to live righteously.

Lord, thank you for taking my life from raggedy to righteous.

May 16
GLAD FOR GRACE

"But by the grace of God I am what I am, and His grace toward me was not in vain; but I labored more abundantly than they all, yet not I, but the grace of God which was with me."

1 Corinthians 15:10

God's grace is amazing. It is the only reason that we are who we are. In the words of Johnathan Bradford, "There, but for the grace of God, go I." The undeserved, unmerited, unwarranted, and un-acquirable grace of God has brought us thus far. It is no wonder that grace is the subject of so many gospel songs. It is at the heart of every believer. I believe that until we truly come to understand grace, we cannot fully appreciate or comprehend God's great love for us. We are glad for grace.

Lord, thank you for your undeserved and unmerited favor toward us.

May 17
LOVE IS A VERB

"Let all that you do be done with love."

1 Corinthians 16:14

Love changes and matures as we mature in Christ. When we are baby believers love is a noun. Love is seen as a person, place, or thing. It is a feeling we experience during worship service. But at this stage in our Christian walk it is not an action word. As we develop and mature, love is no longer a noun, but becomes a verb...an action word. As a seasoned saint, love is no longer about what we receive but rather it is about what we do. Love becomes an action word, a verb. Love is what love does. Love as a verb is a sign of Christian maturity.

Lord, grow my love from a noun into an action word. Let my love be a verb.

May 18
COMFORTED TO COMFORT

"Who comforts us in all our tribulation, that we may be able to comfort those who are in any trouble, with the comfort with which we ourselves are comforted by God."

2 Corinthians 1:4

When Jesus ascended to heaven, He did not leave us alone. He left us with The Comforter, the Holy Spirit. The Comforter is with us in all our tribulation. This is not only for our own comfort, but so that we may be able to comfort others who are in any trouble. Offering comfort to others is an act of Christian kindness. Let us always remember that we have been comforted to comfort.

Lord, you have comforted me in my time of sorrow let me do the same for others.

May 19
PRESSURE MAKES DIAMONDS

"We are hard-pressed on every side, yet not crushed; we are perplexed, but not in despair; persecuted, but not forsaken; struck down, but not destroyed—"

2 Corinthians 4:8-9

Most natural diamonds are formed at high temperature and pressure at depths of 140 to 190 kilometers (87 to 118 mi) in the Earth's mantle. On January 25, 1905, at the Premier Mine in Pretoria, South Africa, a 3,106-carat diamond was discovered during a routine inspection by the mine's superintendent. Weighing 1.33 pounds, and christened the "Cullinan," it was the largest diamond ever found.

The Cullinan was later cut into nine large stones and about 100 smaller ones, valued at millions of dollars all told. Christians are also diamonds. We become most beautiful under the pressures of life. We become most beautiful under the pressures of life. We are hard-pressed on every side, confused and perplexed, persecuted and pained, struggling and struck down. Yet that is only the pressure makes diamonds. In Christ we are not crushed; we are not in despair; we are not forsaken; we are not destroyed. Just diamonds in the rough.

Lord, let the pressures of life make me beautiful.

May 20
EXPECTING THE ETERNAL

"Therefore we do not lose heart. Even though our outward man is perishing, yet the inward man is being renewed day by day. For our light affliction, which is but for a moment, is working for us a far more exceeding and eternal weight of glory, while we do not look at the things which are seen, but at the things which are not seen. For the things which are seen are temporary, but the things which are not seen are eternal."
2 Corinthians 4:16-18

It can be frustrating when others won't join in your pity party. My dad is one of those people. Whenever I have felt the pressures of life squeezing and afflicting me, my dad would often say, "this too shall pass." When I was younger, this would frustrate and anger me. I mean could your one and only child get a little sympathy? Now that I am older, chronologically and spiritually, I have come to understand that my dad knew a truth of faith that I had yet to understand fully. No matter what goes on in our lives, it will pass. Whatever we are facing it is only for a moment. We should, therefore, focus on the eternal.

Lord, remind me daily that whatever I am facing it is but for a moment and it will pass.

May 21
WHEN I CAN'T GOD CAN

"And He said to me, "My grace is sufficient for you, for My strength is made perfect in weakness." Therefore most gladly I will rather boast in my infirmities, that the power of Christ may rest upon me."

2 Corinthians 12:9

When we are burdened with infirmities, our first response is usually to complain, worry, or both. However, as we grow and mature in Christ, we will see our infirmities and our weaknesses as opportunities to completely depend on God. When we are weak, it is an opportunity to depend on God fully. The Bible tells us that God's strength is made perfect in our weakness. Therefore, when we can't, God can. That is good news.

Lord, thank you that your strength is made perfect in my weakness. When I can't, you can.

May 22
GIVE GOD YOUR BEST
"Whatever work you do, do it with all your heart. Do it for the Lord and not for men."
Colossians 3:23 (NLV)

The signature block on my work email is Colossians 3:23. It serves as a daily reminder that whatever I do at work, I should do it with all my heart as for the Lord and not for people. This should be true not only when at work but in whatever I find myself doing. As Christians, we should strive always to give God our best and not our mess. Unfortunately, as Christians, we give our best to our jobs, our family, our friends, even our churches, but we end up giving God only the leftovers which is not our best. We can do everything to the glory of God. Rev. Dr. Martin Luther King Jr. encouraged us to do just that when he said, "If a man is called to be a street sweeper, he should sweep streets even as a Michelangelo painted, or Beethoven composed music or Shakespeare wrote poetry. He should sweep streets so well that all the hosts of heaven and earth will pause to say, 'Here lived a great street sweeper who did his job well...No work is insignificant. All labor that uplifts humanity has dignity and importance and should be undertaken with painstaking excellence." We should give God our best in all that we do.

Lord, let me always give you my best and never my mess. May I strive daily to do everything for your glory.

May 23
CHASING AFTER YOU

"...run away from youthful desires. Instead, direct your passion to chasing after righteousness, faithfulness, love, and peace, along with those who call upon the Lord with pure hearts."
2 Timothy 2:22 (VOICE)

I love to watch my two children chase one another in the backyard. It brings my heart great joy to watch their youthful joy spill over in smiles and laughter as they take turns chasing one another. The scene becomes more moving when the one being chased is caught and therefore receives a gigantic laughing hug from the one doing the chasing. It is a scene that reflects our own spiritual pursuits of God. In this passage in Timothy, we are instructed to flee youthful desires. Once we do that, we can direct our passion toward chasing after the things of God. The things we should be chasing include righteousness, faithfulness, love, and peace. The joy we will find chasing after the things of God will reflect the joy of my children chasing one another and then end up in a loving embrace.

Lord, let me flee the immature desires of my flesh and diligently chase after you with my whole heart.

May 24
CUT ME DEEP

"For the word of God is living and powerful, and sharper than any two-edged sword, piercing even to the division of soul and spirit, and of joints and marrow, and is a discerner of the thoughts and intents of the heart."

Hebrews 4:12

Research has shown that the number of Christians who read the Bible on a daily or even regular basis is dropping at an alarming rate. According to the research, the Word of God does not hold the significance it once held with Christians. The result is stunting their growth. As we grow in God we should understand some divine truths about the Bible:

- The Bible was not written about God; The Bible is God's word.
- The Bible is not a great book; it is a divine book.
- The Bible is the only book that is timeless and remains relevant despite the ages.
- The Bible is how God speaks to us.
- The Bible shows us God's will.

Studying the Bible is essential in the life of Christians. The Bible is living and powerful, it cuts us deep discerning our thoughts and intents.

Lord, lead us to study your word daily so that it can cut us deep.

May 25
BLESSED BOLDNESS

"Let us therefore come boldly to the throne of grace, that we may obtain mercy and find grace to help in time of need."
Hebrews 4:16

As we grow as Christians our view of prayer changes, well it should. Prayer is seen by baby believers as intimidating and ritualistic. As we become seasoned saints, prayer is viewed as a privilege, and we have confidence that our prayers are powerful and effective. Our confidence comes from boldly approaching the throne of grace. Boldness comes from how we A.C.T. as we approach the throne. First, adore the one who sits on the throne. Next, we confess our sins because we don't want anything to stand between us and our prayer requests. Then, we thank God for what He has already done in our lives. Doing these three things gives us the boldness to approach God for whatever we need. This is blessed boldness.

Lord, thank you for the holy boldness to approach your throne to adore you, confess to you, thank you, and make my requests known to you.

May 26
NOW FAITH IS

"The fundamental fact of existence is that this trust in God, this faith, is the firm foundation under everything that makes life worth living. It's our handle on what we can't see."

Hebrews 11:1 (MSG)

Faith is falling without a net beneath you, jumping without a parachute, taking off without wings, and landing in His hands. Faith is essential to the life of Christians. Without it, we cannot please God. Faith is necessary assurance, without it we would fall. Here are a few acronyms about F.A.I.T.H:

F.A.I.T.H. –forward all issues to heaven.

F.A.I.T.H.—full assurance in the heart.

F.A.I.T.H.—forsaking all I trust him.

F.A.I.T.H.—full assurance it will truly happen.

Lord, let me walk by faith and not by sight; may my faith please you and may my faith assure me of the things hoped for and not seen.

May 27
KEEP RUNNING

"Therefore we also, since we are surrounded by so great a cloud of witnesses, let us lay aside every weight, and the sin which so easily ensnares us, and let us run with endurance the race that is set before us,"

Hebrews 12:1

There are many parallels between runners and Christians. Runners all start on the same line and run at their own pace. Christians all begin at salvation and run the race of salvation at their own pace. Fans cheer on runners as they run the race, just as the saints of old cheer on Christians in the heavenly realm. Runners must lay aside any weight that could cause drag during the race. Likewise, Christians should put aside anything or anyone who weighs down our race. Run with endurance. Whether you are a 100m sprinter or marathon runner, you must run the race with endurance. Keep running until the end.

Lord, let me keep my focus on you, running with endurance until the end of the race.

May 28
FOCUSED FINISH

"Looking unto Jesus, the author and finisher of our faith, who for the joy that was set before Him endured the cross, despising the shame, and has sat down at the right hand of the throne of God."

Hebrews 12:2

We need to focus on Jesus. We need to look to Jesus and what He means to us as Christians. Jesus is the author and finisher of our faith. Look to Jesus, focus on what he did. He endured the cross and paid the debt that he did not owe. He paid the debt that we owed. He despised the shame He endured on our behalf and never said a single word to his accusers. Look to Jesus and focus on what he is doing. He now sits at the right hand of the throne of God interceding on our behalf. Interceding for us when we confess our sins. Finally, look to Jesus and focus on what he will do. Jesus is coming again in splendor and glory and takes us to a place with no more pain, sickness, or trouble. We need to focus on Jesus, the author and finisher of our faith.

Lord, you are the author and finisher of our faith, let me always fix my focus on you.

May 29

JOY FOR THE JOURNEY

*"My brethren, count it all joy when you fall into various trials,
knowing that the testing of your faith produces patience.
But let patience have its perfect work, that you may be perfect
and complete, lacking nothing."*

James 1:2-4

One of my favorite gospel songs is *Thank You Lord* by Walter Hawkins. The lyrics speak of the joy in thanksgiving. They state, "Tragedies are commonplace, All kinds of diseases, People are slipping away, Economies down, People can't get enough pay, As for me, all I can say is, Thank you, Lord, for all you done for me." The joy for the journey of life begins with a thankful heart. If we took time to thank God more, our lives would be full of joy. In this life, we will have tests and trials that could cause you to be unhappy. Happiness is based on outward circumstances, but joy is based on salvation on the inside. With Jesus, we can have joy for the journey. With Jesus, we can count every condition where we find ourselves in life as joyful because testing produces patience and patience make us perfect and complete.

Lord, thank you for joy for the journey. No matter what we I'm facing in life, I can still have joy.

May 30
GO SLOW

*"So then, my beloved brethren, let every man be
swift to hear,
slow to speak,
slow to wrath;"*

James 1:19

I have heard my children's preschool teachers often repeat that God gave us two ears and one mouth, we should therefore listen more than we speak. These words are a direct reflection of the words of James. First, he advises us to be quick to hear. We should listen often. If we examine carefully, the giants of faith were avid listeners to God and other Christians. Likewise, we should be slow to speak. Many of the things we are saying are the things we really should be praying. What we often call discussion is just gossip. Finally, we should be slow to anger. As much as we think it is, most situations aren't even about us. It is usually about the person and not you. As Christians, we should go slow...slow to speak and to get angry. We can more easily do this if we are quick to listen.

Lord, let me be quick to listen, slow to speak, slow to anger and quick to pray.

May 31
FIRST THINGS FIRST
"Therefore submit to God. Resist the devil and he will flee from you."

James 4:7

D o you remember the Weeble Wobble toy? My son had one when he was a baby that was a horse. He could push, grab it, hug it, climb on it, but it would not stay down. It would pop right back up time and time again! He enjoyed hours and hours of trying to get that little plastic horse to stay down, but no matter how hard he tried it would always pop back up again. Sometimes it feels like Satan is a weeble wobble. He weebles and wobbles in our lives, wreaking havoc, but he won't fall. This verse reminds us that the devil is defeated and will flee, but there are a couple of things we must do first. We must first submit to God. One reason we can't seem to win against the enemy is that we haven't fully submitted our lives to God. Everyone wants Christ as Savior, but not everyone wants Christ as Lord of their lives. It is the submission that allows us victory over the enemy. Once we submit to God, we can resist the devil and his tricks. Then he will flee. But first things first, submit to God.

Lord, help me to give my life fully committed to you so that I can resist the devil.

JUNE

June 1

THIS HOPE I HAVE

"Instead, you must worship Christ as Lord of your life. And if someone asks about your hope as a believer, always be ready to explain it."

1 Peter 3:15 (NLT)

Worshipping God gives many benefits. One of them in hope. It is impossible to remain optimistic in this world without hope. The Bible speaks about hope in many instances. The dictionary describes hope as a feeling of trust, expectation, and desire for something to happen. As believers, our hope is in God. Our hope is in spending an eternity with Him. When we worship God, our hope in God's plan for our lives increases. Our hope in spending an eternity with God increases. As believers, it is our responsibility to spread this same hope throughout the world. It is impossible to share this hope if we ourselves are not filled with this hope. Today, spend some time in worship. Ask God to restore your hope so that you may share your hope as a believer with others.

Lord, thank you for hope. Restore my hope in you so that I may share your saving power with the world.

June 2
WORRIER TO WORSHIPER

"casting all your cares [all your anxieties, all your worries, and all your concerns, once and for all] on Him, for He cares about you [with deepest affection, and watches over you very carefully]."

1 Peter 5:7 (AMP)

The enemy will allow us to consider so many negative "what if" scenarios that we worry ourselves sick. Worrying can cause us to lose sleep and our peace. Worrying is the result of thinking what could happen to us. It's crazy because there is no way we can be sure of the outcome of our situations. As Christians, we know our outcome. No matter if the outcome is in our favor, we know that it will work out for the good. When we worry, we tell God that our problem is too big for Him to take care of. Worrying is a result of lacking in our faith in God. This 1 Peter passage is one of my go-to scriptures whenever I feel my heart leaning toward worry. Although the passage is referencing worry, it is really about turning worry into worship. Instead of worrying, we should begin to worship God. In our worship, we should thank Him for already taking care of the issues that concern us.

Lord, I can cast my cares upon you because you care for me.

June 3

G.R.O.W.

"But grow [spiritually mature] in the grace and knowledge of our Lord and Savior Jesus Christ. To Him be glory (honor, majesty, splendor), both now and to the day of eternity. Amen."

2 Peter 3:18 (AMP)

When I was growing up, the phrase "you go girl/boy' was trendy. Its use increased when comedian Martin Lawrence used to say it on his hit show "Martin." The phrase is a statement of affirmation to others for a job well done. It is a phrase of praise. One that could be applied to Christians as we GROW in Christ. Each day as we greet the Lord in devotion we grow: Greet the Lord in prayer, Read and study His word, Observe the truth, Walk in His ways. If we do these things daily, we GROW! Take some time today GROWing in the Word of God!

Lord, let me GROW daily in the character of Christ through prayer, study, and walking in your truth.

June 4

OBEDIENCE EVIDENCE

"We know that we have come to know him if we keep his commands."

1 John 2:3 (NIV)

People will know that we belong to God if we keep His commandments. We don't have to wear a "I LOVE JESUS" t-shirt. People will know we are Christians by the love we show others. Jesus tells us throughout the Gospels that the greatest commandment is to love God and the second greatest commandment is to love people. If we love God and people, we can keep all the other commandments. It is our love for God and our love for people that will keep us from being disobedient to God. Obedience to God is all the evidence that we need to show that we have grown in Him! Don't worry about trying to convince people that you have matured in God. Let your OBEDIENCE speak for you.

Lord, let me love you, love others, and keep your commandments.

June 5

CAN YOU HEAR ME NOW

*"Now this is the confidence that we have in Him,
that if we ask anything according to His will, He hears us."*

1 John 5:14

As Christians, we have the assurance that God hears and always answers our prayers. What we struggle with is how He answers our prayers. Sometimes God's answer is an immediate yes, and we receive exactly what we have asked of Him. Other times God answers, but His answer is no, and He does not give us what we have requested. God can also say wait, for either we are not ready for the blessing or the blessing is not ready for us. Whether God says yes, or no, or wait, we can be confident that he hears us. No matter what, we must trust His timing, His will, and His way.

Lord, thank you for hearing and answering our prayers. Help me to trust your timing and your plan for my life.

June 6
PROSPERITY GOSPEL

"Beloved, I pray that you may prosper in all things and be in health, just as your soul prospers."

3 John 2

Prosperity Gospel has taken on an entirely different meaning recently. The focus is far from the soul and sin and more so on health and wealth. So much so that faith has been associated with good health and great wealth. Those who are healthy and wealthy are said to have great faith. The Bible makes a priority of our soul being prosperous. We prosper when our soul prospers. How does our soul prosper? Our souls prosper when we grow closer to God. Our growth happens by taking intentional time to pray, study, and seek God. Our souls prosper when we allow ourselves to be convicted to change. Nothing is wrong with acquiring wealth, however, this must not be more important than becoming spiritually wealthy.

Lord, thank you for prospering our souls, minds, and bodies.

June 7
IN HIS HANDS

"I drew a picture of you on my hand. You are always before my eyes."

Isaiah 49:16a (ERV)

Isaiah, like many other prophetic writers in the Bible, has such an eloquent way with words. I personally love the way they literally illustrate God's unwavering love for us. In the scripture above Isaiah expresses our security in God by saying that He has drawn a picture of us in his hands. What the writer is trying to express is how we are not only constantly in God's view, we are also always in His reach, in His Hand. Take a moment and think about the closeness of something you hold in your hand. This scripture also describes God's intimacy with us. God knows everything about us. He knows every thought we think, word we speak, and action we take. He knows us so intimately. He shaped us in our mother's womb. He has numbered our days, and accounts for the very hairs on our head. God knows what we need and when we need. God made us in his image. We can take comfort knowing that our God has us in the palm of his hands. No matter where we may find ourselves physically and mentally, we can rest assured that we are always in the Master's hands! What assurance we have in knowing that we are never far from our Master's reach!

Lord, my life is in your hands ...literally.

June 8
LOOK WHAT THE LORD HAS DONE

"Look what the Lord has done for me! He decided to help me. Now people will stop thinking there is something wrong with me."

Luke 1:25 (ERV)

E lizabeth, like many other women in the Bible, was barren. She had not given birth. But then God opened her womb! Similarly, many Christians are barren. We have not given birth to the spiritual things God has planted inside us. But then God opens our spiritual womb and takes the barren places of our flesh and transforms them into just what we need. Look what the Lord has done by turning our Trials into Triumph, Tests into Testimonies, Messes into Messages, Victims into Victors, Worriers into Worshipers, and above all Sinners into Saints. Look what the Lord has done!

Lord, thank you for deciding to help me when I couldn't help myself.

June 9
THE GREATEST

*"For God so loved the world, that He gave His only begotten
Son, that whosoever believeth in Him should not perish,
but have everlasting life."*

John 3:16

John 3:16 is what the entire Bible circulates around. The Bible is better than any Harlequin Romance novel. It is truly the greatest love story. From the beginning of time in Genesis, all the way to Revelation and everything in between, we see evidence of God's love for us. The entire Bible is about God's desire to return us to our rightful position in Him. Everything He has done for us is because of His love for us. He washed the Earth clean to purify us…He allowed the fall of great cities. He allowed the enslavement of His chosen people. He allowed His son, His only Son, Jesus Christ to die on the cross. He did this all for us. There is nothing we can do to repay Him for His love for us. What we can do is spend every day in gratitude for Him giving us the greatest gift ever – eternal life.

Lord, thank you for the greatest gift ever, the gift of eternal life.

June 10
Sin Nonsense

"We know that our old sinful selves were crucified with Christ so that sin might lose its power in our lives. We are no longer slaves to sin. For when we died with Christ we were set free from the power of sin. And since we died with Christ, we know we will also live with him."

Romans 6:6-8 (NLT)

No matter how much we try to fix, twist, and justify, sin doesn't make any sense. Sin is anything in direct opposition to God and His word. Sin is separation from God. Sin is walking in our flesh. Doing any of these things is nonsense. It has been said that continuing to do the same thing and expect different results is insanity. Sin is insanity because we expect God not to punish what he has already said he would punish. But we serve a no-nonsense God. When our old sinful nature was crucified with Christ, sin lost its hold on us. We have been set free from the nonsense of sin.

Lord, thank you for setting me free of the nonsense of sin.

June 11

ALL GLORY TO GOD

"You are worthy, our Lord and God, to receive glory and honor and power, for you created all things, and by your will they were created and have their being."

Revelation 4:11 (NIV)

Everyone likes to receive adoration, adulation, accolades, and admiration. However, as Christians, we have learned that in and of ourselves we can do nothing. Everything that is worthy of praise belongs to God. All glory should be given to God. All credit should be given to Christ. Why? Only God is worthy of glory, honor, and praise. We the created must praise the Creator.

Lord, you alone are worthy of glory, honor, and praise.

IF NOT FOR GOD...

"If it had not been the Lord who was on our side..."

Psalm 124:1a

Helen Baylor once wrote lyrics that reflect this Psalm, "If it had not been for the Lord on my side, where would I be? Where would I be?" That is a question that Christians should ponder each day. Where would we be if the Lord had not been on our side? Where would we be if God had not loved us so intimately. Where would we be if God had looked upon our transgressions and decided that we were not worth salvation? I'll make it even more practical for you. Where would you be right now if God was as inconsistent as you are? Where would you be with His love when you felt like you were alone? Where would you be if God had not provided? Where would you be if God had not taken care of your needs? As baby believers, we fail to grasp the significance of having God on our side. But as we continue to walk and talk with Jesus on a regular basis, we grow to understand that if God had not been on our side, there is no telling where we would be.

Lord, thank you for always being there for us.

June 13
FILL ME UP GOD

"So Elisha said to her, "What shall I do for you? Tell me, what do you have in the house?" And she said, "Your maidservant has nothing in the house but a jar of oil."
Then he said, "Go, borrow vessels from everywhere, from all your neighbors—empty vessels; do not gather just a few.
And when you have come in, you shall shut the door behind you and your sons; then pour it into all those vessels, and set aside the full ones."
So she went from him and shut the door behind her and her sons, who brought the vessels to her; and she poured it out.
Now it came to pass, when the vessels were full, that she said to her son, "Bring me another vessel."
And he said to her, "There is not another vessel." So the oil ceased."

2 Kings 4:2-6

Our God specializes in filling empty vessels. We are instructed to come before Him, a full fountain, as an empty vessel. Like the widow with Elijah, we must come before God empty and trust that He will fill us up. First, we must present an empty vessel. If we are full of ourselves or full of things of the world, there is no room for God. Next, we must acknowledge our need. In matters of the spiritual, we can often overlook or ignore our needs. We must acknowledge where there is a spiritual lack in our lives and ask God to fill it. Finally, we should thank God when our needs are met.

Lord, when my vessel is empty fill me up.

June 14
MAKE ME LIKE YOU

"So I went down to the potter's house and saw him working with clay at the wheel.
He was making a pot from clay. But there was something wrong with the pot. So the potter used that clay to make another pot. With his hands he shaped the pot the way he wanted it to be. Then this message from the Lord came to me:
"Family of Israel, you know that I can do the same thing with you. You are like the clay in the potter's hands, and I am the potter." This message is from the Lord."

Jeremiah 18: 3-6 (ERV)

The flesh wants what it wants, and that is for us to be unlike Christ and like the world. It is the Holy Spirit that molds us into the character of Christ. Being shaped into the likeness of God and the character of Christ is a process. The prophet Jeremiah likens it unto a potter working his clay. God is the potter, and we are the clay. The wonderful image encourages us in that whenever the Potter finds something wrong with the pot (us), He continues to shape the pot into what He wants it to be. If we allow Him, He can make us like Him.

Lord, make me like you. Mold me, make me, shape me, like you.

June 15
IN YOUR PRESENCE

"You make known to me the path of life; you will fill me with joy in your presence, with eternal pleasures at your right hand."

Psalm 16:11 (NIV)

My grandparents sang, "I woke up this morning with my mind, stayed on Jesus. Walking and talking with my mind, stayed on Jesus. Singing and praying with my mind, stayed on Jesus. Hallelujah!" They understood the importance of keeping our minds stayed on Jesus. In the presence of the Lord is the fullness of joy. When we fix our focus on Jesus, we remain in His presence. Our actions, our words, and our thoughts will all be better because we are in the presence of the Lord.

Lord, keep my mind stayed on you and make my joy full in your presence.

June 16

STAND OUT DON'T BLEND IN

"And do not be conformed to this world [any longer with its superficial values and customs], but be transformed and progressively changed [as you mature spiritually] by the renewing of your mind [focusing on godly values and ethical attitudes], so that you may prove [for yourselves] what the will of God is, that which is good and acceptable and perfect [in His plan and purpose for you]."

Romans 12:2 (AMP)

Christians were not born to blend in; we were born to stand out. However, everything around us tells us to blend in or go along to get along. How do we stand out when the world we live in tells us to blend in? We are instructed to be transformed, that is to mature spiritually by focusing on the things of God. Transformation is a process. It does not occur overnight. It is not a quick, fast, in a hurry occurrence. In fact, maturation is a slow, deliberate, and focused happening. We were not born to blend in. We were born to stand out.

Lord, thank you for making me, choosing me, setting me apart to stand out.

June 17

SEE AND WAIT

'Call to Me and I will answer you,
and tell you [and even show you] great and mighty things,
[things which have been confined and hidden],
which you do not know and understand and cannot distinguish."
Jeremiah 33:3 (AMP)

The world tells us to wait and see. However, as Christians we walk by faith and not by sight. This allows us to do exactly the opposite of what the world would advise us to do. As Christians, we see (believing) and then wait to watch God move. We pray believing that God hears and will answer our prayers. We know that God is answering even when we can't see Him moving. By faith, God will allow us to see the answers to our prayers before He sends the answers. This is a blessing of walking and praying in His will. Forget wait and see, we see and wait.

Lord, thank you for always answering when I call.

June 18
CONFESSION IS CRITICAL

"If we confess our sins, he is faithful and righteous to forgive us our sins and to cleanse us from all unrighteousness."

1 John 1:9 (HCSB)

There is a familiar quote that says, "confession is good for the soul." However, it is critical to the life of Christians. If we confess our sins, God is faithful and just to forgive us our sins and clean us up and make us whole. It is with confession that the work of salvation begins and that we move into a relationship with Jesus Christ. Confession is critical in the life of seasoned saints. Not the blanket confession of baby believers, "Lord, forgive my sins." Mature confession, naming our sins individually, or better yet, repenting as soon as we sin. Not waiting until bedtime to repent of what we have thought, said, done, or left undone. In the life of a Christian, confession isn't good for the soul, it is critical.

Lord, thank you for forgiving my sins and hearing my confessions.

June 19
TIME AND CHANGE

"There is a time for everything, and a season for every activity under the heavens"

Ecclesiastes 3:1 (NIV)

There are many familiar quotations on change.

"The only thing constant in life is change."

"The more things change, the more they stay the same."

No matter how much we long for stability, life is dynamic. Our children are born, our parent's die. We get our dream job, our company downsizes. We fall in love; we get divorced. Life changes and the Bible tells us there is a season for every activity under the sun. The good news is that there is one other constant besides change in life and that is God. God is with us when our children are born and when our parent's die. God is with us when we are hired and when we are fired. God is with us when we fall in love, and when we are divorced. God is with us all the time and through every change.

Lord, continue to walk with me through the changes of life and remind me that you are with me in every season of life.

June 20
CALL HIM UP

"I will call on Him as long as I live, because He has turned His ear to me."

Psalm 116:2 (NLV)

Whitney Houston was one of the greatest singers of all times. While I enjoy her pop hits, my all-time favorite song is her rendition of "I Love the Lord." When she sings,

"I love the Lord
He heard my cry
And pitied every groan
Long as I, I live
And troubles rise
I'll hasten to his throne."

She is boasting the words of the 116th Psalm. In it, we are reminded that God has turned His ear to us. Therefore, we will call on Him. When life is hard, we will call on Him. When life is easy, we will call on Him. When we are hurting, we will call on Him. When we are healed, we will call on Him. As long as we live, we will call on the Lord.

Lord, thank you for always turning your ear towards me. Allow me to call on you forever.

June 21

ANOTHER CHANCE

"Forgive as the Lord forgave you."

Colossians 3:13b (NIV)

Forgiveness is difficult. If we look at it in light of how God forgives, it becomes easier. While we struggle to forgive after one wrong, God faithfully forgives us over and over. He is not the God of a second chance, but rather He is the God of another chance...and another chance...and another chance. When we are reluctant to forgive others, we need look no further than how quickly we want God to forgive us. As God is quick to forgive us, we should be quick to forgive others.

Lord, lead me to forgive others as you have forgiven me.

June 22
MAKE IT PERSONAL

"I will meditate on Your precepts and [thoughtfully] regard Your ways [the path of life established by Your precepts]. I will delight in Your statutes; I will not forget Your word."

Psalm 119:15-17 (AMP)

Scripture and prayer go hand in hand. Reading God's word and praying God's word are both essential to Christian growth. Reading scripture during our prayer time makes our prayers more personal. Furthermore, scripture can be used when we cannot form the words to say in our prayers. When we don't know what to say, we can say scripture. When we want to make it personal, pray scriptures.

Lord, thank you for your word and allowing me to pray your word back to you.

June 23

COMPLETE IN CHRIST

"So when Jesus had received the sour wine, He said, "It is finished!" And bowing His head, He gave up His spirit."

John 19:30 (NKJV)

The Bible tells us in John 10:18 that no one took Jesus' life but instead, He laid it down freely. It is this awesome power that completed the work of salvation on the cross. By Jesus deciding to die in our place, we are now complete in Christ. "It is finished." The work of salvation is complete. There is nothing more to be done. Nothing that we can do. We can only receive the gift of salvation and share the gift of being complete in Christ.

Lord, we are complete in you; let us share that truth with others.

June 24
SO MUCH MORE

"Jesus did many other things as well. If every one of them were written down, I suppose that even the whole world would not have room for the books that would be written."

John 21:25 (NIV)

J ust as John wrote the world could not retain the records of all Jesus did, how many volumes could we write ourselves? Just think of your own life, whether you are twenty, forty, or eighty. How many wonderful things has God done in your life? How many things has He kept us from? Dangers seen and unseen? How many ways has He made? How many doors has he opened? God saved us when we were sinking deep in sin. He thought of us when we couldn't have cared less about Him. God is keeping us, even when we can't keep ourselves. God has done all this—and so much more!"

Lord, thank you for all the numerous wonderful things you have done in my life.

June 25
PLUG IN

"But you shall receive power when the Holy Spirit has come upon you; and you shall be witnesses to Me in Jerusalem, and in all Judea and Samaria, and to the end of the earth."

Acts 1:8

A power source is essential in our modern lives. Our technology requires that we plug into a power source daily. From computers to tablets, to phones—all require being plugged in to be effective. It is the same for our spiritual lives. To work properly, we must be plugged into the ultimate power source. We receive power when we receive the Holy Spirit; Holy Ghost Power.

Lord, thank you for empowering me to be your witness.

June 26
BETTER TOGETHER

"All the believers were together and had everything in common."
Acts 2:44 (NIV)

I t seems one of the enemy's greatest tools, especially among Christians is division. Satan knows if he can divide us, then he can conquer us. He works diligently to create division through gossip, distrust, and misunderstanding. However, the Bible tells us that believers were together and had everything in common. If we are of one mind and have other things in common, things will be better together.

Lord, help me to work diligently to promote unity and not division.

June 27

NO OTHER NAME

"Salvation is found in no one else, for there is no other name under heaven given to mankind by which we must be saved."

Acts 4:12 (NIV)

There is a place in our souls that only God can fill. Rick Warren calls it our "God-shaped space." Unfortunately, society tells us that there are many roads to God and that we can give God a piece of our heart. The world encourages us to use retail therapy, children, and careers—but nothing can fill this void. That God-shaped space is reserved for God alone. We spend much of our lives seeking for things to fill us. After every purchase, relationship, job, and church, we still find ourselves empty. The reason why is because nothing can fill this void but God. The things the world offers us can only satisfy us temporarily. They give us the illusion of wholeness, but they don't make us whole. They can't complete us because they didn't make us. The only one who can fill our void is our Creator, the Most High God.

Lord, thank you for being the only way to salvation and for filling my God-shaped space.

June 28
DOING LIKE DORCAS

"In Joppa there was a disciple named Tabitha (in Greek her name is Dorcas); she was always doing good and helping the poor."

Acts 9:36 (NIV)

As baby believers we tend to be all about self. We are selfish and self-righteous, but as we mature our acts of love and good works should grow as well. We have a wonderful example of a Christian in Dorcas. The Bible tells us "she was always doing good and helping poor." The fact that she was always doing good and helping the poor is an example of Christian maturity. As we mature in our walk, we should also become more selfless. Take some time today and do something selfless!

Lord, let me be like Dorcas. Help me to be less about self and more about helping others.

June 29
FEELS LIKE THE FIRST TIME

"and when he found him, he brought him to Antioch.
So for a whole year Barnabas and Saul met with the church and
taught great numbers of people. The disciples were called
Christians first at Antioch."

Acts 11:26 (NIV)

D o you remember the first time you were called a Christian? Better yet, do you remember when you first became a Christian? Were you a child? A teen? An adult? No matter, when or where or what type, our conversion experience should be one we never forget and one we should always be ready to share. I once heard that our testimony should be like an elevator speech. We should be able to share our testimony and Jesus before someone steps on and off an elevator with us. Every time we share our testimony, it should feel like the first time we were saved.

Lord, let me never forget when I was saved and let me always be ready to share.

June 30
ENCOURAGE

*"When he arrived and saw what the grace of God had done,
he was glad and encouraged them all to remain true to the Lord
with all their hearts. He was a good man, full of the Holy Spirit
and faith, and a great number of people were brought to the
Lord."*

Acts 11:23-24 (NIV)

Let's be honest for a second. This Christian race is NO JOKE. Sometimes, people make the mistake of thinking that when we sign up to follow Christ, our lives immediately become void of disappointments, heartbreaks, and trials. This couldn't be further from the truth. The truth of the matter is that our "yes" to God is an immediate threat to the enemy. He knows that if we grow stronger in God, his attacks and tactics will be useless. For this reason, the enemy begins to throw so many obstacles on our path. The crazy thing is, God allows them! God allows them so that we will be strengthened, and so that His Glory can be revealed in us and through us. Every testimony of what we have endured can be used to encourage our sisters and brothers in Christ.

Today, think about how your testimony can encourage others. Have you gone through financial struggles and know a sister or brother who is going through a financial storm of their own? Set aside a few minutes to share your testimony and encourage them that God is going to work everything out for the good! Encourage someone today!

Lord, let me encourage others.

JULY

July 1
BEYOND ME

"For my thoughts are not your thoughts, neither are your ways my ways," declares the Lord. "As the heavens are higher than the earth, so are my ways higher than your ways and my thoughts than your thoughts."

Isaiah 55:8-9 (NIV)

Our understanding is finite, but God is infinite. Our ways are limited to the natural, while God's ways are supernatural. Our thoughts are ordinary, but God's ways are extraordinary. As baby believers, we believe, but we need God to help our unbelief. As we grow with God, our finite becomes infinite. Our natural becomes supernatural, and our ordinary becomes extraordinary. This takes time, trials, and tribulations. It's when the rubber meets the road that we experience God's infinite wisdom. There's nothing like watching God work out a situation that we thought was impossible. Not only does He work it out, but He does it in such a way that others are able to see. No one does it quite like God! While we may not understand His ways, we can be sure that His ways are definitely more creative and beneficial than our own. My prayer today is that God will blow your mind and show you just how "out of the box" He is!

Lord, I'm glad you are not like me.

July 2
MY BURDEN BEARER

"Praise be to the Lord, to God our Savior, who daily bears our burdens."

Psalm 68:19 (NIV)

As human beings, we often try to bear the weight of the world on our own. The world views individuality and self-sufficiency as a strength. It tells us that asking for help is a sign of weakness. The old hymn of the church says "I know He's a burden bearer. I know He's a heavy load sharer…" This song sings the words of Psalm 68. God is our burden bearer. Whatever burdens we bear, God will help us bear them. We are not in our struggles alone, however, many times it feels this way because we refuse to take our burdens to God. We refuse to allow him to work in our lives. We refuse to ask Him for the strength we need to carry everything He has placed on our shoulders. God equipped us by giving us His Spirit. As long as His spirit lives in us, we will not fall under the weight of the responsibility of being a child of God!

Lord, thank you for being a burden bearer and a heavy load sharer.

203

July 3
MY FORTRESS

"I will love You, O Lord, my strength.
The Lord is my rock and my fortress and my deliverer; My God,
my strength, in whom I will trust; My shield and the horn of my
salvation, my stronghold."

Psalm 18:1-2 (NIV)

What is a fortress? The dictionary defines a fortress as a heavily protected and impenetrable building. In the scripture above, the Psalmist describes the Lord as his fortress. Sometimes, the storms of life hit us back to back. It can often feel as if we are exposed to the climate of the world. However, when we love the Lord, He is our fortress. When the winds blow, we can run to Him and be safe. He will shield us and protect us. When people try to destroy our reputation, His love covers us. When we are down to our last and don't know what to do, He provides for us. There is no storm that can penetrate God's protection. He is a fortress! A Fortress! Today, if you begin to feel overwhelmed, turn to God and allow Him to protect you from the hits hell may attempt to send your way.

Lord, thank you for protecting me from all hurt, harm, and danger.

July 4

ACT NOW

"Keep actively watching and praying that you may not come into temptation; the spirit is willing, but the [a]body is weak."
Matthew 26:41 (AMP)

Prayer is an action word. When we pray, we A.C.T. **A**dore God. **C**onfess our sin. **T**hank God. We don't want anything to hinder our prayer ACTion, but some things can hinder our prayer. Reading about prayer, but failing actually to pray can hinder our prayer lives. When we do not confess our sins, we hinder our prayer lives. When we allow grudges to dwell in our hearts, we hinder our prayer lives. When we don't take the faith steps God commands us to take, we hinder our prayer lives. Today during your prayer time, be sure that you ACT!

Lord, lead me to remember that prayer is an ACTion word.

July 5
CRY OUT

"Hear my cry, O God; Attend to my prayer. From the end of the earth I will cry to You, When my heart is overwhelmed; Lead me to the rock that is higher than I. For You have been a shelter for me, A strong tower from the enemy. I will abide in Your tabernacle forever; I will trust in the shelter of Your wings."

Psalm 61:1-4

When we are overwhelmed, our first reaction in our flesh is to curse. Some of us are pretty good at it as well. Ever heard of a cussing Christian? As we mature in Christ, our first reaction should become to cry out to God. We can seek the security of God by learning to cry out. When in doubt, cry out. The reason why we instantly say curse words, is because we have filled ourselves with the filth of the world instead of the richness of God's Word. As a result, when we are squeezed, dirty things come out. To ensure that God's word's come out of us during the press, we have to study God's Word in season and out of season. As you fill yourself with God's Word, you will properly be able to speak to the storms of life when they hit!

Lord, when I am overwhelmed, let me cry out to you.

July 6
WAIT

"Wait on the Lord; Be of good courage, And He shall strengthen your heart; Wait, I say, on the Lord!"

Psalm 27:14

Waiting is not easy especially in a world of instant gratification, Instagram and instant coffee. The world seemingly moves at the speed of imagination, but this is not always true with the things of God. Although God can answer sooner than right now and faster than immediately, sometimes, He says, "Wait." We are in good Biblical company as we wait:

- Joseph waited 13 years.
- Abraham waited 25 years.
- Moses waited 40 years.
- Jesus waited 30 years.

The Bible even tells us what to do while we wait. We are to be of good courage and wait. While we are waiting, God will strengthen our hearts.

Lord, you are the strength of my heart while I wait.

July 7
POWER OF GOD'S LOVE

"Who shall separate us from the love of Christ? Shall tribulation, or distress, or persecution, or famine, or nakedness, or peril, or sword? As it is written: "For Your sake we are killed all day long; We are accounted as sheep for the slaughter." Yet in all these things we are more than conquerors through Him who loved us. For I am persuaded that neither death nor life, nor angels nor principalities nor powers, nor things present nor things to come, nor height nor depth, nor any other created thing, shall be able to separate us from the love of God which is in Christ Jesus our Lord."

Romans 8:35-39

The power of God's love is seen throughout Romans 8. In this scripture in particular, we gain reassurance that nothing can separate us from the love of God. Sometimes, the enemy's tactics are to pull us away from God's love from us. The thing is, even though we may be tempted to no longer trust, love, and believe in God, He will never stop loving us. Absolutely nothing can separate us from His love. God's love for us is greater than the love we receive from our earthly parents. Our earthly parents love us so much that they will go to any depths or heights to save us, but there are some places that they cannot reach. God's love can reach us wherever we are. Where are you? Do you feel as if you are far from God's love? Spend some time in prayer recommitting yourself to Him and welcoming Him into your heart. God is waiting for you!

Lord, your love is powerful, and it protects me. Thank you for never allowing anything, not even me, to separate me from your love!

July 8
SPRINKLE KINDNESS

*"Be kind and helpful to one another, tender-hearted
[compassionate, understanding], forgiving one another [readily
and freely], just as God in Christ also forgave you."*
Ephesians 4:32 (AMP)

Allow me to tell you a short story about kindness. An eighty-two-year-old's chance encounter with a four-year-old little girl in a grocery store blossomed into a beautiful friendship. The four-year-old introduced herself in the store and told the gentleman that it was her birthday. She proceeded to hug him and take a selfie with him. This simple act of kindness became so much more. The act of kindness has bloomed into a beautiful friendship. The eighty-two-year-old called her his angel.

We never know what people are going through. We should be diligent in sprinkling kindness wherever we go. Our simple act may be the only kindness people experience that day.

**Lord, let us always show others the loving kindness you have
shown us.**

July 9
IT'S YOUR TIME

"For if you remain completely silent at this time, relief and deliverance will arise for the Jews from another place, but you and your father's house will perish. Yet who knows whether you have come to the kingdom for such a time as this?"

Esther 4:14

As baby believers, we often ask, "Why me Lord?" We question everything that comes our way. But as we grow we come to accept that God works all things together for good. We begin to understand that sometimes God allows things "for such a time as this." We are exactly where God wants us to be so He can use us for His purposes. The point is not to benefit us personally, but to bless others. Whatever we are currently facing, who knows, God may have ordained it exactly "for such a time as this."

Lord, remind us that we may be where we are for such a time as this.

July 10

ABIDE

"And may love the Lord your God, obey His voice, and cling to Him. For He is your life and the length of your days..."

Deuteronomy 30:20 (AMPC)

The dictionary defines abide as "obey, follow, hold to, stick to, standby, act by, uphold, heed, accept, go along with, acknowledge, respect, defer to." Cling is defined as "hold on to, clutch, grip, grasp, clasp, attach oneself to, hang on to." The Bible instructs us to do both. Cling to God. Abide in Jesus. How do we cling and abide? To cling, we are instructed to love God and obey Him. Loving God keeps our focus on Him. Obeying God keeps our heart with him. Clinging keep us in relationship with Him. We know we are abiding in Christ by the fruit we bear.

Lord, let me cling, grasp, hold tight, to you and abide, remain in Jesus.

July 11

CHOSEN

"You did not choose Me, but I chose you and appointed you that you should go and bear fruit, and that your fruit should remain, that whatever you ask the Father in My name He may give you."
John 15:16

Aren't you glad that you have been chosen by Jesus? When we were lost in sin, He chose us. When we weren't thinking about Him, He chose us. When we couldn't choose properly for ourselves, He chose us. God has chosen us and appointed us to produce fruit. Only what we do for Christ will last. Since Jesus chose us, we should keep choosing Him.

Lord, thank you for choosing me, appointing me, and allowing me to bear fruit.

July 12
DELIGHT IN DIFFICULTIES

"And not only that, but we also glory in tribulations, knowing that tribulation produces perseverance; and perseverance, character; and character, hope. Now hope does not disappoint, because the love of God has been poured out in our hearts by the Holy Spirit who was given to us."

Romans 5:3-5

Many passages in the Bible at first glance appear hypocritical. "We glory in tribulations," what? Other translations say, "we rejoice" or "we brag" or "we boast" in our tribulations. Now, why should we do that? I should be sad, depressed, upset when things don't go my way, right? Wrong! The Bible tells us to glory because of the end result of tribulation. Through tribulation we become able to persevere. Perseverance develops character and character produces HOPE— having only positive expectations. Hope does not disappoint.

Lord, help me to glory in trouble in order to persevere, develop character, and have hope.

July 13

GOD'S GRACE

"And He said to me, "My grace is sufficient for you, for My strength is made perfect in weakness." Therefore most gladly I will rather boast in my infirmities, that the power of Christ may rest upon me."

2 Corinthians 12:9

There are numerous gospel songs about grace, "Amazing Grace," "Thank You For Your Grace," and the recent hit by Luther Barnes "God's Grace." I love the lyrics. They state, "How did I make it all these years? How did I make it this far? Through the valleys and over the hills, I know it had to be God. How did I make it through the storm? How did I make it through the rain? If you want to know, just how I got here, it's so easy to explain. It was God's grace, I made it this far, by the grace of God." God's grace keeps us, sustains us, it is sufficient. Grace is God's unmerited favor toward us. It is getting what we do not deserve. Grace is my redemption at Christ's expense. Grace gives me SWAG—saved with amazing grace. God's grace!

Lord, thank you for your undeserved, unmerited favor—grace!

July 14

STRENGTH IN WEAKNESS

"Therefore I take pleasure in infirmities, in reproaches, in needs, in persecutions, in distresses, for Christ's sake. For when I am weak, then I am strong."

2 Corinthians 12:10

One of the worst feelings in the world is being ill and not getting any relief. Before being properly diagnosed with fibroids, this is exactly how I felt. But through prayer and God's word, I learned to worship when I was weak. I learned to show integrity when insulted and to care for others when I was in catastrophe. I learned how to be pleasant in persecution and how to praise under pressure. I learned how to rejoice in reproach and delight in distress. I learned how to be happy in hardships and calm in calamity. There is so much strength in our weakness. For when we are weak, we find our strength in the Lord. If we had never had infirmities, reproaches, needs, persecutions, or distress, we would never know the strength God gives in weakness.

Lord, when I am weak, you are my strength.

July 15
DON'T WORRY

"Don't worry about anything; instead, pray about everything. Tell God what you need, and thank him for all he has done. Then you will experience God's peace, which exceeds anything we can understand. His peace will guard your hearts and minds as you live in Christ Jesus."

Philippians 4:6-7 (NLT)

I t has been said, "If you are going to pray, why worry and if you are going to worry, why pray?" Bobby McFerrin said, "Don't worry, be happy." Stevie Wonder said, "Don't you worry 'bout a thing." Life can cause us to worry, but the Bible admonishes us not to worry about anything but to pray about everything. We can tell God all about our concerns, He already knows about them anyway. Then, Paul instructs us to thank Him for what He has already done—that's praise. When we thank Him, we are giving Him the praise that is due Him. As a result, His peace will guard our hearts and minds. So don't worry. Pray.

Lord, remind me not to worry about anything, but to pray about everything.

July 16
TO DO LIST

"Always be joyful. Never stop praying. Be thankful in all circumstances, for this is God's will for you who belong to Christ Jesus."

1 Thessalonians 5:16-18 (NLT)

I believe in making "to do" lists daily, monthly, and annually. My planner (yes, I still use a print planner in addition to Outlook) is full of reminders and post it notes. With all that is going on in our lives, the lives of our family and the lives of our friends, we are so busy that we often make the things of God secondary instead of a priority. Reading, praying, and applying the Word of God should be at the top of our "to do" lists. When they are not priorities, we feel the consequences. We must make it a priority on our "to do" list to be joyful, consistent in prayer, and thankful.

Lord, I want you to be the priority in my life.

July 17
PRECIOUS PROMISES

"By his divine power, God has given us everything we need for living a godly life. We have received all of this by coming to know him, the one who called us to himself by means of his marvelous glory and excellence. And because of his glory and excellence, he has given us great and precious promises. These are the promises that enable you to share his divine nature and escape the world's corruption caused by human desires. In view of all this, make every effort to respond to God's promises.
Supplement your faith with a generous provision of moral excellence, and moral excellence with knowledge, and knowledge with self-control, and self-control with patient endurance, and patient endurance with godliness, and godliness with brotherly affection, and brotherly affection with love for everyone."

2 Peter 1:3-7 (NLT)

God has given us everything we need to live godly lives. He did this when we first accepted Christ. Because of what God has done we should "make every effort to respond to God's promises." Faith leads to goodness, which leads to knowledge, which leads to self-control, which leads to endurance, which leads godliness, which leads to the brotherly affection which, leads to love. Love is the perfect way. What precious promises God has given us. Let us respond accordingly.

Lord, thank you for giving us everything we need to live a godly life.

July 18
FREEDOM IS FREE

"Therefore if the Son makes you free, you are free indeed."
John 8:36 (NKJV)

People can be the worst when you are trying to turn over a new leaf. Sometimes, when we try to change for the good, those closest to us constantly bring up who we once were. It's like they won't give us the chance to change! No worries. The reason people do this is because they have not completely forgiven us for the things we may have done wrong. Our job is not to be concerned with the forgiveness habits of others. If you have truly repented, God has already forgiven you. In fact, He expects you to change and transform regardless of how bad your transgressions were. Paul was a murderer. He murdered Christians for most of the early part of his life. However, after his encounter with God on Damascus, he was transformed and began to share the Gospel of Jesus Christ. Can you imagine how many people looked at him crazy? Can you imagine how frustrating it was for Paul to try to promote to those same people the very thing he spoke against? Yes, it may have been hard for Paul, but He kept pushing towards the mark. Our scripture today reminds us that when we have been set free by the Son, we are truly free! If you have accepted salvation, you are free! Don't worry about what people say. Pray that they will find forgiveness in their hearts and keep it moving! You are free indeed!

Lord, please help me as I try to live a life that is more pleasing to you!

July 19
A CLOSER WALK

"They seized Him, led Him away, and brought Him into the high priest's house. Meanwhile Peter was following at a distance."
Luke 22:54 (HCSB)

Staying close to Jesus is critical. Distance is a tool and trick of the enemy for doubt and spiritual decline. If we want to continue to grow in Christ, we must walk closely with Him. Peter shows us what happens when we follow at a distance. We are quick to deny Him. It is much more difficult to deny someone who you are up close and personal with. A closer walk with Jesus is just what we need.

Lord, let me walk closely with you to decrease doubt and grow in grace.

July 20

PRAYER ROOM

"But when you pray, go into your room, close the door and pray to your Father, who is unseen. Then your Father, who sees what is done in secret, will reward you."

Matthew 6:6 (NIV)

In the scripture above, Jesus was instructing the disciples on the best practices of prayer. In those times, the Pharisee, Sadducees, and other religious rulers would go outside in their long robes and say eloquent prayers aloud so that others could marvel at their ability to pray. Jesus advised the disciples not to pray in this manner. He told them to pray in their secret place. This does not mean that we should not participate in corporate prayer. When we do pray, we must not pray for the approval of others, instead we must pray for the attention of God. Additionally, our prayer in private is what gives us the ability to pray for others in public settings. We gain our strength in prayer through the private prayers we pray alone with God. Since the movie, *Prayer Room*, was released, everyone has been cleaning out their closets to set it aside as a prayer room. Nothing is wrong with this, however, if you don't have the extra space to designate as a prayer room, don't feel bad. Pick a quiet space in your home to pray and seek God.

Lord, let me purpose daily to spend time in prayer and studying your word.

July 21
NO SHAME IN MY GAME

"And they overcame him by the blood of the Lamb and by the word of their testimony, and they did not love their lives to the death."
Revelation 12:11 (NKJV)

D o you have any idea how powerful your testimony is? You may not be aware of it, but you can bet your bottom dollar that hell knows the power of our testimony. When we experience trials and tribulations, the first thing we sometimes feel is shame. We are afraid for anyone to find out what we have gone through. We become concerned with what people will think about us. Here's the thing, our testimonies have the power to not only change our lives, but also the lives of others. Think about it like this: Not everyone knows the word of God. In fact, most people who are unsaved don't believe in the Bible, and they definitely don't want to spend time listening to someone rant on and on about a bunch of scriptures that don't mean anything to them. Do you want to know what their ears would be inclined to? Hearing a real life testimony of someone who has been where they are! Sometimes, we are afraid to share the stories of our clubbing, drinking, smoking, inconsistent, poor money management, or fornication days. However, if we are to save the people who are still in the ways of the world, we must be able to relate to them! The scripture says that not only did they overcome by the Blood of the Lamb, but also by the word of their testimonies! Don't be afraid to share your testimony with others! Your story just might be the story they need to hear to turn their lives over to Christ!

Lord, give me the boldness to share my testimony with those who need to hear it!

July 22
JUST BE CONTENT

*"Not that I speak in regard to need, for I have learned in
whatever state I am, to be content:"*

Philippians 4:11

We are in a time when media screams at us to accumulate more and more. Secular music seduces us with, "Don't stop get it get it" or "Get money" or "It's all about the Benjamins, baby." Its message is in direct opposition to the word of God. No wonder people, including some Christians, are never satisfied. In the scripture above, Paul says that he learned what it means to be content! Being content does not mean that we don't have needs or desires. Being content means that we have learned how to be happy and grateful for what we have and where we are. Despite what we may be dealing with, contentment allows us to still be grateful, happy, and satisfied. When we learn the secret of contentment, life becomes a lot less stressful! We no longer feel the pressure to compete with the Joneses! Learn the secret of contentment today.

Lord, teach me to be content with whatever I have.

July 23
LISTEN CLOSELY

"My child, pay attention to what I say. Listen carefully to my words. Don't lose sight of them. Let them penetrate deep into your heart, for they bring life to those who find them, and healing to their whole body."

Proverbs 4:20-22 (NLT)

The Oprah effect refers to the effect that an appearance on the Oprah Winfrey Show or endorsement by Oprah Winfrey can have on a business. From Weight Watchers to books to movies, everything Oprah touches seems to turn to gold. It has made her among the most influential African Americans in our Nation's history. People live by her words. Many people including Christians heed her words as gospel. However, we are advised in Proverbs to heed the word of God. We treasure them in our heart because they are life and healing. While listening to Oprah may be a great endorsement. Listening to God is the greatest endorsement.

Lord, let me listen closely, and then heed, keep, and trust your Word.

July 24
WORDS TO LIVE BY

"for in Him we live and move and have our being..."

Acts 17:28a

One of my favorite old hymns of the church speaks the truth of Acts 17:28, "I can't live in this world without the Lord. I can't live in this world without the Lord. When I look around and see what the Lord has done for me. I can't live in this world without the Lord." The next verse says "I can't raise my right hand without the Lord." Another verse says, "I can't bow on my knees without the Lord." This depends on who Christ is to you. Charles Spurgeon said, "If Christ is not all to you He is nothing to you. He will never go into partnership as a part Savior of men. If He is something He must be everything, and if He is not everything He is nothing to you." We truly cannot live, move, or pray without the Lord.

Lord, I can't live, move, or be without you.

July 25
GOD IN ME

"I have been crucified with Christ and I no longer live, but Christ lives in me. The life I now live in the body, I live by faith in the Son of God, who loved me and gave himself for me."

Galatians 2:20 (NIV)

Gandhi once said," I like your Christ, I do not like your Christians. Your Christians are so unlike your Christ." That is a powerful indictment. Consider that as Christians, we look nothing like Christ in the way we talk, the way we behave, or the way we think. At the point of salvation, we take off the old man and put on the new man. It is no longer we who live but Christ lives in us. The old man along with our old ways have been put to death. They no longer live in our body. By faith and the great love of Christ, we can do this. It is no longer us, but the God in us that others see. Let us be holy representatives.

Lord, my old self is dead, Christ lives in me.

July 26

AFTER WHILE

"In his kindness God called you to share in his eternal glory by means of Christ Jesus. So after you have suffered a little while, he will restore, support, and strengthen you, and he will place you on a firm foundation."

1 Peter 5:10 (NLT)

'm so glad, trouble don't last always. This too shall pass. Joy comes in the morning. These are common Christian clichés that we lean on in times of trouble. Whatever trouble we are facing in our lives we can take heart; the Bible promises us that trouble doesn't last always. After a while ,we will be restored. After a little while, we will be supported. After a little while, we will be strengthened. We will be restored. We will be placed on a firm foundation. So chin up, shoulders back, and back straight. It will all be over after a while.

Lord, thanks for the assurance that trouble don't last always.

July 27

FIGHT THE FLESH

"The acts of the flesh are obvious: sexual immorality, impurity and debauchery; idolatry and witchcraft; hatred, discord, jealousy, fits of rage, selfish ambition, dissensions, factions and envy; drunkenness, orgies, and the like. I warn you, as I did before, that those who live like this will not inherit the kingdom of God."
Galatians 5:19-21 (NIV)

We are in the fight of our lives daily. We go to blows over the behaviors of our bodies. Although obvious when we read them in the Bible, these behaviors often sneak into our lives undetected. They are subtle until they come to dominate areas of our life. To fall into such behaviors is sin, but to live in them places a wedge between God and us. We must, therefore, fight the flesh daily.

Lord, when my flesh fails me fortify my faith.

July 28
ADDED FLAVOR

"Therefore, as we have opportunity, let us do good to all people, especially to those who belong to the family of believers."

Galatians 6:10 (NIV)

When did kindness become so rare and unheard of that it gets its special news segment? Special reports on kindness are rare between stories on road rage, crimes of passion, internet trolling, hate speech and the like. Kindness is rare. As Christians, we should always seek to leave others sprinkled with kindness. It should be added flavor from being in our presence.

Lord, as you are kind toward us, let us be kind to others.

July 29
BUT NOTHING

"But because of his great love for us, God, who is rich in mercy, made us alive with Christ even when we were dead in transgressions—it is by grace you have been saved."
Ephesians 2:4-5 (NIV)

How many times have we been interrupted with, "but nothing" by a parent or grandparent? The phrase leaves us hurt and unsure. However, in the Bible the phrase "but God" is the greatest interruption possible. BUT ...God...two words that always make all the difference in any given situation. Throughout the Bible the words "but God" precede God interfering on behalf of His people. But as for you, you meant evil against me; but God meant it for good, in order to bring it about as it is this day, to save many people alive (Genesis 50:20). BUT GOD will redeem my soul from the power of the grave, For He shall receive me (Psalm 49:15). My flesh and my heart fail; BUT GOD is the strength of my heart and my portion forever (Psalm 73:26). BUT GOD demonstrates His love toward us, in that while we were still sinners, Christ died for us (Romans 5:8).

Lord, thank you for interrupting our life circumstances.

July 30

TOO DEEP, TOO WIDE

"so that Christ may dwell in your hearts through faith. And I pray that you, being rooted and established in love, may have power, together with all the Lord's holy people, to grasp how wide and long and high and deep is the love of Christ, and to know this love that surpasses knowledge—that you may be filled to the measure of all the fullness of God."

Ephesians 3:17-19 (NIV)

So high, you can't get over it.
So wide, you can't get around it.
So low, you can't get under it.
How can we describe the love of Christ? We can't. When we think about the love of God, it is beyond our comprehension.

Lord, your love for me is long, high, and wide.

July 31
START WITH SUBMISSION

"Submit to one another out of reverence for Christ. Wives, submit yourselves to your own husbands as you do to the Lord. Children, obey your parents in the Lord, for this is right. "Honor your father and mother"—which is the first commandment with a promise—"
Ephesians 5:21-6:2 (NIV)

A Christian home starts with submission. We have a problem with submission because we have yet to submit to God. Both spouses submit to God. Next, wives submit to husbands. If your spouse has submitted to God, then submission to them should not be an issue. Finally, children obey parents. Finally, if both parents submit to God, the wife submits to the husband, the children will obey because they see obedience modeled in the submission of their parents. Obedience and submission is modeled from the head down.

Lord, let me view submission with new appreciation.

AUGUST

August 1
NOT MY SIZE

"So Saul clothed David with his armor, and he put a bronze helmet on his head; he also clothed him with a coat of mail. David fastened his sword to his armor and tried to walk, for he had not tested them. And David said to Saul, "I cannot walk with these, for I have not tested them." So David took them off."

1 Samuel 17:38-39

In the story of David and Goliath, there is a moment where Saul attempts to prepare David for his battle against Goliath. In his attempt to prep David, he gives David his armor. Saul's armor did not fit David. It was not sized for him. Can you imagine what would have happened if David attempted to go into battle wearing Goliath's armor? He would have been tripping over his shield, and probably constantly readjusting his helmet so that he could see. Wearing Saul's armor would have distracted David for sure. So many of us are losing in our life's battles because we are trying to walk in things that were not fit for us to wear. Instead of being who God has called us to be, we sometimes seek to be like our parents or other people around us. Like David, God has a specific purpose and plan for our lives, though it may appear to be similar to the paths of others, it is not alike. We must be sure to put on the careers, relationships, and connections that God has for us to put on. Don't allow others to live vicariously through you, additionally, don't attempt to live vicariously through others. Be content with the path God has chosen for you and walk in it boldly!

Lord, show me the plan you have for my life. Give me the strength and desire to walk in it!

August 2
ONLY ONE

"No one can serve two masters. Either you will hate the one and love the other, or you will be devoted to the one and despise the other. You cannot serve both God and money.

Matthew 6:24 (NIV)

t is impossible to love this world, and love God. Point. Blank. Period. Right now there are Christians who believe that they can love and participate in the things of this world, and still please God. Here's the thing, God doesn't force us to love Him, but He makes it clear that we must make a decision. We cannot have Him and the world. We must chose to serve God with everything in us, in everything that we do, and everywhere we go. We cannot lift our hands in church and the club! We must CHOOSE this day who we will serve! The scripture above reminds us that when we have two masters, we will love one and hate the other one. The world causes us to sin, and go against the ways on God. God hates sin, and when we choose Him, we too learn to hate sin and the sinful ways of the world. Do you see how it works? Make up your mind to be sold out for the Lord!

Lord, help me to daily choose you!

August 3

GOD'S GOT ME

"being confident of this, that he who began a good work in you will carry it on to completion until the day of Christ Jesus."
Philippians 1:6 (NIV)

The Urban Dictionary defines "I got you," as "I got your back," "I got you covered," or "I got you protected." Whatever God has begun in our lives, He is faithful to complete it. That dream or ministry God is leading us in, He will work it to completion. We can be confident in whatever it is that God is doing, He will complete. People will say they have our backs, but flake on us when times get tough. Not God! He is committed to your well-being and your success. Even when other fail you, rest assured that God's Got Your Back!

Lord, let me never forget that you've got me!

August 4

SQUAD GOALS

"I thank my God every time I remember you. In all my prayers for all of you, I always pray with joy"

Philippians 1:3-4 (NIV)

"Squad goals" is an inspirational term for what we'd like our group of friends to be or accomplish. Unfortunately, we often epitomize the wrong groups as squad goals, or we admire certain squads for the wrong things. Before you set a group of individuals as your squad's goals, be sure that they epitomize God's righteousness! In the scripture above, Paul expresses his adoration and love for the people of Philippi. We should be careful to find friends and leaders who think of us in the same way!

Lord, thank you for praying friends, accountability partners, and iron sharpening friends.

August 5

NOT ABOUT US

"Let each of you look out not only for his own interests, but also for the interests of others."

Philippians 2:4

The world is selfish. It tells us "look out for yourself," "watch your back," "go solo," "trust no one," "I am the captain of my soul," "me, myself, and I." The dictionary defines selfish as being "egocentric, egotistic, self-centered, self-absorbed, self-obsessed, self-seeking, self-serving, wrapped up in oneself; inconsiderate, thoughtless, unthinking, uncaring, or uncharitable." We are even told to let others "pull themselves up by their own bootstraps." As Christians, we are advised to look for the interests of others. When we fix our focus on Christ, he allows us to fix our focus on others; what they need, how we can encourage them, their well-being, we realize that it is not about us at all. Joy will be a priority—Jesus, others, and yourself.

Lord, remind me it's not us, it's about J.O.Y.

August 6
JUST TO KNOW HIM

"I want to know Christ—yes, to know the power of his resurrection and participation in his sufferings, becoming like him in his death,"

Philippians 3:10 (NIV)

How has just knowing Jesus Christ changed your life? Many Christians have not witnessed change in their lives because they have signed up to follow Christ, but have not committed to learning about Christ. When we learn about Jesus Christ and His ways, we are encouraged to live more like Him. Many have not changed because they don't know what they should because they don't know Christ. In your study time, challenge yourself to highlight the traits of Jesus Christ and embody them in your life.

Lord, thank you for the privilege of just to knowing you. Show me more of your traits so that I may learn how to live.

August 7
PRESS

"Not that I have already obtained all this, or have already arrived at my goal, but I press on to take hold of that for which Christ Jesus took hold of me. Brothers and sisters, I do not consider myself yet to have taken hold of it. But one thing I do: Forgetting what is behind and straining toward what is ahead, I press on toward the goal to win the prize for which God has called me heavenward in Christ Jesus."

Philippians 3:12-15 (NIV)

I f we want an abundant life with Jesus, we must press. Forget the past, press toward what is ahead.
Press, like Joseph, past disappointment.
Press, like Moses, past oppression.
Press, like Paul, past persecution.
Press, like Mary, past haters.
Press, like Thomas, past doubt.
Like a runner, we must press toward the goal. Not allowing the past to stop us. We must press beyond our past toward the goal set before us.

Lord, help me to push beyond my past and press toward my future.

August 8
WON'T HE DO IT?

"And now to him who can keep you on your feet, standing tall..."
Jude 2:4 (MSG)

We serve a God that turns our trials into triumph, our mess into a message, our fear into faith, and our tests into testimonies. However, many feel as though their testimony isn't worth sharing. I was once like this. I didn't feel as though my testimony was "powerful" enough to share and lead others to Christ. I accepted Christ at the age of eight, and I have been walking closely with Him ever since. I never strayed far and felt this was not the testimony that others wanted to hear. If this is you, be encouraged every salvation testimony is a story for glory. Our God can save from the guttermost to the uttermost, but more than that. God can keep that which is His. Jude reminds us that God can keep us from stumbling or falling. I'm a witness, won't He do it?

Lord, thank you for being able to keep me from falling or stumbling.

August 9
I COME IN PEACE

"Pursue peace with all people, and holiness, without which no one will see the Lord;"

Hebrews 12:14

Some people are just DIFFICULT. That's just the truth of it. They make it hard to love them or even want to be around them. HOWEVER, the writer of Hebrews admonishes us to try our best to live at peace with all people. Sometimes, this requires us to be the bigger person and put our pride to the side. Sometimes, this requires us to smile when we feel like yelling to the top of our lungs. This is what we are required to do as Christians. Sometimes, all it takes for an individual to change their attitudes is the love of Christ. Be that love today!

Lord, help me to be at peace with everyone you place on my path!

August 10
BE HUMBLE OR STUMBLE

"And whoever exalts himself will be humbled, and he who humbles himself will be exalted."

Matthew 23:12

C.S. Lewis said, "True humility is not thinking less of yourself; it is thinking of yourself less." Mother Teresa gave us practical ways to practice humility, "Speak as little as possible of one's self. Mind one's own business. Do not want to manage other people's affairs. Avoid curiosity. Pass over the mistakes of others. Accept insults and injuries, being slighted or forgotten or disliked. Be kind and gentle even under provocation." If we are not humble, we will trip over our own egos. If we do not humble ourselves, we will stumble.

Lord, keep me humble so that I do not stumble.

August 11
R.A.S.K.

"A kind answer soothes angry feelings, but harsh words stir them up."

Proverbs 15:1 (CEV)

When I was in college, it was popular to have R.A.S.K. (random acts of simple kindness) or A.S.K. (acts of simple kindness) jars. These are glass jars filled with colorful strips of paper that each describe a small act of kindness. Daily you select one strip of paper and perform the act written on it. There are scientifically proven benefits of being kind. According to the Random Acts of Kindness website kindness is teachable and contagious. Kindness decreases pain, stress, anxiety, depression, blood pressure. The Bible describes the power of kindness. It tells us a kind answer soothes anger. Perform random acts of simple kindness daily and watch angry feelings flee.

Lord, let my actions always be kind and let me show kindness to others.

August 12
LOVE GOD, LOVE PEOPLE

"So he answered and said, " 'You shall love the Lord your God with all your heart, with all your soul, with all your strength, and with all your mind,' and 'your neighbor as yourself.'"

Luke 10:27

There are two types of relationships in our lives: vertical and horizontal. Both are important. Our horizontal relationships are those with our family, friends, co-workers, fellow church members, etc. Our vertical relationship is with God. We should work diligently to guard both relationships. The way we do that is with love. We cannot get our horizontal relationships right if we don't first get our vertical relationship right. If we first love God with all our heart, soul, strength, and mind, then we can love our family, friends, and neighbors as ourselves.

Lord, let me love You with all my heart, soul, strength, and mind so that I can love others as myself.

August 13
RUN FOR YOUR LIFE

"Flee sexual immorality. Every sin that a man does is outside the body, but he who commits sexual immorality sins against his own body."

1 Corinthians 6:18

The Bible is particular about how we are to deal with sexual immorality. It tells us to flee. Synonyms for fleeing include run away, dash, take flight, be gone, make off, take off, make a break for it, bolt, make a quick exit, make one's getaway, or escape. When it comes to sexual immorality, the Bible is very clear—run for your life. Whether we are single or married, we are to flee sexual morality. Single Christians are to guard against sexual immorality. They can watch where they go, guarding against getting themselves in compromising situations. The same with us married Christians. The enemy is no respecter of persons; he will try to place married Christians in compromising situations also. So what is a Christian to do? Flee, run for your life!

Lord, let me keep me my body pure for your purposes.

August 14

FRIENDS AND FRAMILY

"Friends love through all kinds of weather, and families stick together in all kinds of trouble."

Proverbs 17:17 (MSG)

One writer said, "Deep friendships are born in the light, but grow up in the dark." True friends shine their light in the dark places of life – cry with us when a parent dies, hold our hand when we lose a child, encourage us when we lost a job. They hug, call, text, and write for no reason at all other than to let us know that they love us and they care. These are the special people, the good friends that become like family, so we call them "framily." The friends you choose to be family. At the other end of the spectrum, we have "frenemies." So-called friends who act more like enemies. They are absent in the darkness of life. They don't make you better but bitter. According to Jennifer Dukes Lee, framily walk in when frenemies walk out. Framily lifts us up when frenemies tear us down. Framily celebrate you while Frenemies compete with you. Framily prays for you while frenemies prey on you.

Lord, thank you for my friends turned family.

August 15
NO LONGER BITTER, BETTER

"Put aside all bitterness, losing your temper, anger, shouting, and slander, along with every other evil. Be kind, compassionate, and forgiving to each other, in the same way God forgave you in Christ."

Ephesians 4:31-32 (CEB)

Bitterness can fester inside of us like an illness. In fact, the Mayo Clinic reports that harboring negative emotions creates a chronic state of anxiety. There are physical and spiritual benefits to moving beyond bitterness. It can lead to healthier relationships, less anxiety, less stress and less hostility, lower blood pressure, fewer symptoms of depression, stronger immune system, and improved heart health. How do we do put aside bitterness and short tempers and anger other evil that creeps into our lives? We are to be kind, compassionate, and forgiving. If we do unto others as God has done unto us through Christ, we will put aside bitterness.

Lord, thank you for making me better not bitter.

August 16

THE ONLY JESUS THEY SEE

"I have been crucified with Christ and I no longer live, but Christ lives in me. The life I now live in the body, I live by faith in the Son of God, who loved me and gave himself for me."

Galatians 2:20 (NIV)

Some people will never step foot inside of a church building. Others will never read a Bible printed or electronic. However, they will still be reached and drawn by the love of Jesus Christ. How you say? By observing the lips and lives, words and actions of the Christians they encounter each day. We may be the only Jesus some people ever see. We may also be the only Bible some people ever read. Therefore, let our actions be covered in the love of Christ and let our words speak the love of Christ.

Lord, let me be a reflection of you with my lips and my life in case I'm the only Jesus someone ever sees.

LaDonna Michele

August 17
GOT ME PRAISING DAY AND NIGHT

"It is good to give thanks to the LORD, and to sing praises to Your name, O Most High; To declare Your lovingkindness in the morning, and Your faithfulness every night,"

Psalm 92:1-2

When I think about the goodness of the Lord and all he has done for me—I can't help but praise. God has been so good to us. Waking each morning is enough reason to praise. If we would simply take the time to think of His goodness toward us; praise will not be far behind. The elders had a clear understanding of thanksgiving, and it could be heard each time they prayed. Like the psalmist, we should give thanks to God day and night for his loving kindness.

Lord, thank you for my portion of health and strength, thank you for a right frame of mind, thank you for the activity of my limbs, thank you for a roof over my head, and floors under my feet. I can't stop praising you for all you have done for me!

Lord, I just can't thank you enough, let your praise be continually in my mouth.

August 18
LIVING TO THE FULLEST

"The thief does not come except to steal, and to kill, and to destroy. I have come that they may have life, and that they may have it more abundantly."

John 10:10

Don't get it twisted or be confused. Our enemy—the father of lies, the thief, he comes only to steal, kill, and destroy. But Jesus came to give us an abundant life. All believers have life through Christ Jesus, but not all believers are living abundantly. Too many Christians are living beneath our means. An abundant life is one lived with abundant spiritual resources that come from our relationship with Jesus Christ. Failing to live abundantly opens the door for us to yield to our flesh. A carnal life is one that is circumstance-controlled while an abundant life is one that is Spirit-controlled. While a carnal life is a defeated life, an abundant life is victorious. According to the Christian Life New Testament, an abundant life is "yielded, serving, separated, spirit-filled, and mature." With these resources, it is possible to live life to the fullest.

Lord, let me live life abundantly, to the fullest, using the abundant resources in Christ.

August 19
SELFIE-LESS

"Instead of each person watching out for their own good, watch out for what is better for others."
Philippians 2:4 (CEB)

The rise of the cell phone camera brought with it the emergence of the "selfie." According to the Pew Research Center, Millennials have taken more selfies than any generation with Gen X in a distant second with 24%, Boomers at 9%, and the Silent 4%. In fact, half of all US adults have taken a selfie (go ahead and snap one while you read this devotion #ReadPrayGrow365). Selfie was added to the Oxford Dictionary in 2013. A selfie is someone who takes a picture of themselves. We now live in a world where selfies have taken on a selfish tone and moved us more towards self-centeredness. How can we combat a selfie driven society and turn it into an usie society? Usie is defined as someone who takes a picture of themselves with other people. According to Crosswalk.com we can learn how to be truly empathetic by thinking about others, sharing the credit, taking the blame, and tying our self-worth to Jesus. When we do these things, we become less selfie-focused and more God-focused.

Lord, let me focus less on me and more on you.

August 20
MAKE ROOM FOR JESUS

"And she brought forth her firstborn Son, and wrapped Him in swaddling cloths, and laid Him in a manger, because there was no room for them in the inn."

Luke 2:7

I t is very frustrating when we are seeking a hotel room and cannot locate one. We search and search only to see that the dates we need are not available. The rejection of there not being any room for us. This is also true in our spiritual lives. The difference is that we are the ones who either make room for Jesus or tell him there is no room available for Him. Like the innkeeper, we tell Jesus all the time that there is no room available for Him. Thanks but no thanks Jesus, I got this. We need to make room for Jesus in our homes, on our jobs, in our churches, but most of all in our hearts. We should make room for Him.

Lord, let me always make room for you in my life.

August 21
AIM HIGH

"Set your mind on the things that are above, not on the things that are upon the earth. "

Colossians 3:2 (ASV)

First Lady Michelle Obama said in her speech during the 2016 Democratic National Convention, "When they go low, we go high." As Christians, we need to keep our minds "stayed on Jesus." Wake up each morning with our mind, stayed on Jesus. Sing and pray with our minds stayed on Jesus. Walk and talk with our minds stayed on Jesus. Hallelujah! This can be fairly difficult in modern times. The pressures of career, family, friends, church, and other activities can disrupt our focus. One of the most powerful weapons the enemy uses against us is distraction. He knows if he can distract us we will lose our focus. But if we can keep our focus on things above and not things of the Earth, if we aim high we will be blessed.

Lord, let me keep my focus on you and not be distracted by things of the Earth.

August 22
PRAYING THROUGH PROBLEMS

"Also, seek the peace and prosperity of the city to which I have carried you into exile. Pray to the Lord for it, because if it prospers, you too will prosper."

Jeremiah 29:7 (NIV)

When we face problems, it can be easy to lose focus. While our flesh tells us to focus on the problem, our spirit should focus on God. We should pray for peace and prosperity during the problem. If our problems are caused by people, we can pray for the peace and prosperity of them as well. For God tells us in His word that when we pray for people causing our problems, He will prosper them and us, We should not focus on the problem, but rather focus on the Problem Solver. Seek God in prayer. Pray through the problem.

Lord, whenever problems arise in my life, let my first response be to pray through the problems.

August 23
NO NOT ONE

"Seeing then that we have a great High Priest who has passed through the heavens, Jesus the Son of God, let us hold fast our confession. For we do not have a High Priest who cannot sympathize with our weaknesses, but was in all points tempted as we are, yet without sin. Let us therefore come boldly to the throne of grace, that we may obtain mercy and find grace to help in time of need."

Hebrews 4:14-16

The hymn writer said, "There's not a friend like the lowly Jesus, No, not one! No, not one! None else could heal all our soul's diseases, No, not one! No, not one! Jesus knows all about our struggles; He will guide till the day is done; There's not a friend like the lowly Jesus, No, not one! No, not one!" Jesus can not only sympathize with our weaknesses, He models what it means to be tempted but not to yield to temptation. Because Jesus knows all about the struggles we face on a day to day basis, we can approach Him in prayer and trust that He will hear and answer our prayers.

Lord, thank you for sending your son who sympathizes with us.

August 24
LORD, LIFT US UP

"Humble yourselves in the sight of the Lord, and He will lift you up."

James 4:10

Bebe and CeeCee Winans sang in 1984, "Lord, lift us up where we belong..." Christians are motivated to achieve. We strive to live up to the descriptors of strong and independent. Unfortunately, when we are trying to climb the professional ladder, we can allow the ways of the world to creep in as well. When the world says, "pull yourself up by your bootstraps," Christ says, "you can do all things through Him." When the world says, "If you aren't first you are last," Christ says "finish the race." When the world says "go hard or go home," Christ says He will lift us up. As Christians, we can be assured that promotion comes from God, He will lift us up where we below.

Lord, lift me up where I belong, elevate me to where you would have me to be.

259

August 25
S.W.A.G.

"Then he called for a light, ran in, and fell down trembling before Paul and Silas. And he brought them out and said, "Sirs, what must I do to be saved?" So they said, 'Believe on the Lord Jesus Christ, and you will be saved, you and your household.'"

Acts 16: 29-31

Merriam-Webster defines "swag" as "sway." In slang terms, "swag" is to walk with confidence and to sway or influence. There are many Christian acronyms for S.W.A.G as well, "someone who adores God," "simply worship almighty God," and "saved with amazing grace." The last acronym is particularly meaningful. We are saved by amazing grace. We were once like the Philippian jailer, completely without S.W.A.G. But then we were introduced to Jesus. We were then saved by amazing grace. Now we have S.W.A.G.—someone who adores God.

Lord, you gave me S.W.A.G. when you saved me with amazing grace.

August 26
YOU KNOW BETTER

"Remember, it is a sin to know what you ought to do and then not do it."

James 4:17 (NLT)

Knowledge of God and His desires come with a great responsibility. We can't just store knowledge of His ways in our minds, we must ACT on them. In the scripture above, James simply lets us know that when we know better, we should do better. This simple principle should be applied in every area of our lives. It's not just enough to know what needs to be done in our lives. We must be intentional about actually doing it!

Lord, help me to apply my knowledge to my life through actions.

August 27

THINK BEFORE YOU SPEAK

"Finally, brothers and sisters, fill your minds with beauty and truth. Meditate on whatever is honorable, whatever is right, whatever is pure, whatever is lovely, whatever is good, whatever is virtuous and praiseworthy."

Philippians 4:8

My grandfather would say there are two things you can never get back, a missed opportunity and a spoken word. In the digital age, it is more critical than ever to THINK before you speak or post or tweet. Is it...True? Is it truthful? A half-truth is a lie. Helpful? Will others be helped or harmed by this? Inspiring? Is it good and praiseworthy? Will it edify others? Necessary? Is this something that needs to be shared? Kind? Would anyone perceive this as unkind? If I cannot "T.H.I.N.K." through something, I shouldn't speak it, or post it, or tweet it or share it. As Christians, it is essential to T.H.I.N.K. before you speak.

Lord, fill my mind with beauty and truth so that I always T.H.I.N.K. before I speak.

August 28
CONSIDER THE CROSS

" [looking away from all that will distract us and] focusing our eyes on Jesus, who is the Author and Perfecter of faith [the first incentive for our belief and the One who brings our faith to maturity], who for the joy [of accomplishing the goal] set before Him endured the cross, [b]disregarding the shame, and sat down at the right hand of the throne of God [revealing His deity, His authority, and the completion of His work]."

Hebrews 12:2 (AMP)

When we truly come to understand the significance of the cross as the cornerstone of Christianity, it changes everything. The hymn writer said, "Jesus is the cornerstone." Indeed He is. The world would like to distract us and lead us to believe that there are multiple ways to get to God. However, we know that Jesus is the cornerstone. He alone is the author and finisher of our faith. Jesus is one brings our faith into maturity. Jesus endured the cross on our behalf. He paid the debt that he did not owe. We should never forget and always consider the cross.

Lord, let me focus my attention on the sacrifice Jesus made just for me on the cross.

August 29
HEART TROUBLE

"Let not your heart be troubled; you believe in God, believe also in Me.

John 14:1

In this world we will have trouble, Jesus told us that. Unfortunately, many Christians have believed the lie of a trouble-free life in Christ. False teachings have confused Christians into thinking that if they live holy enough, give enough, or pray enough trouble will not come their way. The truth, in fact, is that the closer we get to God, the more the enemy will attack us. Trouble is inescapable in this life. However, we can be hopeful. Jesus has promised to be with us through the problems of life. We need not have heart trouble; we have Jesus.

Lord, thank you for walking with me through the troubles of life and continue to keep my heart from being troubled.

August 30
MY DESIRES

"One thing I have desired of the Lord, that will I seek: That I may dwell in the house of the Lord. All the days of my life, to behold the beauty of the Lord, and to inquire in His temple."

Psalm 27:4

We seek after a lot of things in life—love, happiness, careers, etc. All of these things are good, but when we pursue these things we should not lose sight of the main thing—God. We have to work to keep the main thing the main thing. We have to seek after God and the things of God on a daily basis. That should be our desire. When we do this, we can behold the beauty of the Lord.

Lord, let my desire be to chase after you always.

265

August 31
WE CAN ONLY IMAGINE

"But as it is written: 'Eye has not seen, nor ear heard, nor have entered into the heart of man. the things which God has prepared for those who love Him.'"

Corinthians 2:9

I once heard a preacher say some of us will get to heaven and receive our reward. Then God will say, but I had all this prepared for you too, but you failed to trust and obey. When we fail to love God, put him first, trust and obey him, we miss out on so much. The Bible tells us that we haven't seen or heard or imagined the things which God has prepared for those who love Him. Let us trust and obey so that we can walk and receive everything that God has planned for us.

Lord, thank you for preparing great things for me through Christ.

SEPTEMBER

September 1
HOLD ON TIGHT

"Let love be without hypocrisy. Abhor what is evil. Cling to what is good."

Romans 12:9

The dictionary defines "abhor" as "regard with disgust and hatred; loathe, despise." We are told to abhor evil. This is deeper than dislike. When it comes to evil or sin, we are to loathe and despise it. It should repulse us. Or the other hand, we are to cling to what is good. That is to say, hold on to with all that is within us. When we fail to do one or the other, we make our Christianity appear hypocritical. We must do both, and we cannot do one without the other. Then our love will be without hypocrisy.

Lord, let me always shun evil and cling to what is good so that my Christian love will not be hypocritical.

September 2
WHATEVER

"Finally, brothers and sisters, fill your minds with beauty and truth. Meditate on whatever is honorable, whatever is right, whatever is pure, whatever is lovely, whatever is good, whatever is virtuous and praiseworthy."

Philippians 4:8 (VOICE)

There is nothing more annoying than a person to respond "whatever" to a question you have asked. "Where would you like to eat? Whatever." "What movie would you like to see? Whatever." In these instances, "whatever" is flippant and non-concerned. In the Philippians passage however, "whatever" is very specific. It is broadly specific about what Christians are to meditate on. To meditate means to concentrate deeply on something. The Bible is very specific on what we are to meditate on the honorable, right, pure, lovely, good, virtuous, and praiseworthy.

Lord, let my "whatever's" be whatever you want them to be.

September 3
TGIF—TODAY GOD IS FIRST

"But seek first the kingdom of God and His righteousness, and all these things shall be added to you."
Matthew 6:33

TGIF takes on special meaning on Fridays. Workers everywhere breathe a sigh of relief and say together (Thank God It's Friday). But there is another meaning of TGIF—Today God Is First. God must be the priority in our lives, but so often we put so many other things before the Lord. Career, spouse, children, family, and friends often take precedence over God in our lives. Not always intentionally, but gradually we make God and the things of God less of a priority. The Bible tells us to seek the kingdom of God first, and everything we need will be provided. Today God Is First—TGIF!

Lord, lead me to seek you first today and every day.

September 4
YOU WILL HAVE TO ANSWER FOR THAT

"And I tell you that on Judgement Day, people will be responsible for every carless thing they have said."
Matthew 12:36 (NCV)

I don't mean to scare you or anything, but when Judgement Day comes, we will have to stand before God and answer for EVERYTHING we've done. Yes, that means we will have to answer for the gossip, the negative words we said, and also the mean things we said to our brothers and sisters. Though it may seem like we get away with certain things now, one day, we will have to answer for it. Make it a point to only allow positive things to flow from your lips. Remember, one day, you will have to answer for everything you said! Do you really want to have to explain yourself to God?

Lord, help me to be cautious about the words I allow to come out of my mouth.

September 5

GIFT OF GRACE

"Through this man we all receive gifts of grace beyond our imagination."

John 1:16 (VOICE)

We are quick to yell that life isn't fair when things do not go the way we want them to go. The problem is, if life were fair, we would get what we deserve: death. The cost for our sins is death. Grace is getting what we do not deserve. Through Jesus, we have received an incredible gift of grace. So the next time you prepare to fix your lips to say that life isn't fair, turn your phrase around and shout, "God I thank you that life isn't fair!"

Lord, thank you for your incredible gift of grace through Jesus.

September 6

GOD SPECIALIZES

"So the impossible is possible with God."

Luke 1:37 (VOICE)

There are situations, relationships, and obstacles in life that are impossible. God takes our impossible, and with Him, it becomes I'm possible. In fact, the impossible, improvable, and impassable are God's specialties. It is good news that what seems impossible, improvable, and impassable is not so with God. They become I'm possible, I'm provable, and I'm passable.

Lord, when life seems impossible, remind me that's your specialty.

275

September 7
IN THE BEGINNING GOD

"In the beginning God created the heavens and the earth."

Genesis 1:1

In the beginning, God created the heavens and the earth. We spend so much time worrying about endings, however, our God is the God of beginnings. At the beginning of time, He spoke the world into existence. Verse 3, Then God said, "Let there be light"; and there was light. Verse 6, Then God said, "Let there be a firmament....Verse 9 Then God said, "Let the waters under the heavens be gathered together into one place, and let the dry land appear...Verse 11 Then God said, "Let the earth bring forth grass...Verse 14 Then God said, "Let there be lights in the firmament of the heavens to divide the day from the night... Verse 20 Then God said, "Let the waters abound with an abundance of living creatures...Verse 24 Then God said, "Let the earth bring forth the living creature according to its kind...God saved the best for last. Verse 26 Then God said, "Let Us make man in Our image, according to Our likeness...The final creation of God was man. We were in the beginning of creation with God and God continues to begin new things in our lives if we would only surrender and allow him to do so.

Lord, you are the God of beginnings so I don't have to worry about the endings.

September 8

WHAT IS IN A NAME

"And the disciples were first called Christians in Antioch."

Acts 11:26c

I t is not what you are called but what you answer to. Many people call themselves Christians but continue to answer to names of their past lives before Christ. We answer to mom/dad, wife/husband, sister/brother, auntie/uncle, granny/grandad, god-mommy/god-daddy, or cuz. We also answer names that are a lot worse. We should return to when we were first called Christians. As baby believers, we are still struggling with the names we answered to before life with Christ. As we become seasoned saints, we move to answer to what God calls us. We are Christians.

Lord, thank you for saving me and calling me your child.

September 9
WORDS FROM THE HEART

"A good man out of the good treasure of his heart brings forth good; and an evil man out of the evil treasure of his heart[a] brings forth evil. For out of the abundance of the heart his mouth speaks."

Luke 6:45

What is in our hearts comes out of our mouths. Hate speech, love talk, careless whispers—though it comes from our lips it originates in our hearts. Out of a good heart good things, Christ-like things come forth. While an evil heart brings forth evil.

Lord, fill my heart with good treasure and let my lips speak of good things from my heart.

September 10
NEVER WOULD HAVE MADE IT

"This I recall to my mind, therefore I have hope. Through the Lord's mercies we are not consumed, because His compassions fail not."

Lamentations 3: 21-22

Never would have made it without you." Marvin Sapp released a song that sings to the reality of our lives. Try as we might, we never would have made it without God. The fact we are still standing is nothing less than a miracle. Mahalia Jackson sang "my soul looks back in wonder, how I got over." The fact we are still standing is nothing less than a miracle. Because of the mercy of God we are still alive.

Lord, I never would have made it without you; because of you I have hope, and I am not consumed because of your new mercies.

September 11
IT HAD TO DIE

"It was in the year that King Uzziah died that I saw the Lord. He was sitting on a lofty throne, and the train of His robe filled the Temple."

Isaiah 6:1(NLT)

I'm sorry to be the bearer of bad news, but relationships and connections in your life just had to die. You didn't realize it at the time, but they were keeping you from being all that you were created to be. They were keeping you from seeing the Glory of God in your life. So, instead of spending time crying over the people the left you, the jobs you got fired from, the schools you didn't get accepted to, thank God that He allowed everything to happen the way He saw fit.

Lord, give me the strength to thank you and praise your name even when I don't understand.

September 12

SERVED

"For even the Son of Man did not come to be served, but to serve and to give his life as a ransom for many."

Mark 10:45

Many people feel that service is dead. We are so self-centered that most of our focus is on getting served. However, as Christians we are called to be like Christ. Christ came to serve, not to be served. We should look for opportunities to serve others. When we serve we are most like Christ.

Lord, let me be like you, willing and able to serve.

281

September 13
VICTORS NOT VICTIMS

"But thanks be to God, who gives us the victory through our Lord Jesus Christ."
1 Corinthians 15:57

We can have a lot of things thrown our way on a daily basis. We are challenged in our relationships where issues of trust, honesty, and envy rise. We are tried by children, both our own and others as disobedience, rebellion, and bad decisions wreak havoc on their lives. We are stressed by our jobs that push us to our limits professionally and mentally. We are busy at church serving in ministry. We could become victims of our circumstances and cry "why me" all day, but as Christians, we know that we are victorious through Christ. Only our God turns victims into victors. Whatever comes our way we are victorious through Christ, who loves us.

Lord, let me never forget that I am victorious through Christ Jesus.

September 14
HOW MUCH I LOVE YOU

"But God demonstrates His own love toward us, in that while we were still sinners, Christ died for us."

Romans 5:8

Love should never be a question for Christians. In fact, a familiar hymn says, "They'll know we are Christians by our love." Love is the evidence of Christ in our lives. How? When we were still sinking in sin, Christ died for us as a demonstration of God's love. We, therefore, love others because of the great love that God demonstrated toward us. God showed us how much He loved us when he was hung high and stretched wide on the cross. His outstretched arms said, "I love you this much."

Lord, let me always remember how much you love me.

September 15
OVER THERE

"There the wicked cease from troubling, and there the weary are at rest."

Job 3:17

As Christians, we are troubled by the wicked, restless from worry, tears from crying, death, sorrow, and pain. We turn on the news and all we see is bad news. Our online news feeds are full of sad stories from all over the nation and world. It is all almost overwhelming. As Christians, we need not be overwhelmed by the troubles and sorrows of this life. There will be a time free from trouble, a time of rest, no more crying, dying, sorrow, or pain. There is a place where we will forever be at rest with Jesus.

Lord, let me focus my attention on the sacrifice Jesus made just for me on the cross and trust knowing that there is a place prepared for me free of sorrow and pain.

September 16
HELP!

"God is our refuge and strength, a very present help in trouble."
Psalm 46:1

A long traditional prayer is not always necessary or even possible. We can find ourselves in situations where we do not have time to utter but a few brief words. A car cuts us off in traffic, Jesus! We have more month than money, Jesus fix it! We find ourselves at the end of our rope, holding on with one hand, Help! Just because a prayer is brief, doesn't mean it is not as effective as a long prayer. God is our refuge. He is our strength. He is our help when we find ourselves in trouble. Help! That is a mighty good prayer.

Lord, "help!"

September 17
IT ALL STARTS AND ENDS HERE

*"I am the Alpha and the Omega, the Beginning and the End,"
says the Lord, "who is and who was and who is to come, the
Almighty."*

Revelation 1:8

God knows the end from the beginning because he is the beginning and the end. Everything begins and ends with God. He formed us in our mother's womb and then He restored us through Christ. Our beginnings and endings are with God, yet He has no beginning or end. God was, is, and ever shall be. From everlasting to everlasting, our God is. We can rest in knowing that the all-existent God has our lives in His hands.

Lord, remind me daily that everything begins and ends with you.

September 18
HEAVEN ON EARTH

"After these things I looked, and behold, a great multitude which no one could number, of all nations, tribes, peoples, and tongues, standing before the throne and before the Lamb, clothed with white robes, with palm branches in their hands, and crying out with a loud voice, saying, 'Salvation belongs to our God who sits on the throne, and to the Lamb!'"

Revelation 7:9-10

C hrist calls all people, from all over the world to salvation. We may not look alike, talk alike, or worship alike, but what we have in common is our worship of the true and living God who has redeemed us. What will heaven be like? While there are details we do not know, we do know it will be gathering of all God's children. Everyone from everywhere that has accepted the good news of salvation through Jesus Christ will praise God throughout eternity. Imagine that. People from all over the world, all walks of life, all nations, all languages, will be praising the Lord together! I can only imagine.

Lord, I fix my focus on heavenly praise and fellowship with the saints here on earth.

September 19
SONSHINE

"The city had no need of the sun or of the moon to shine in it, for the glory of God illuminated it. The Lamb is its light."
Revelation 21:23

Into each life, some rain must fall." Our God allows His rain to fall on all His children, those by creation and by salvation. Thankfully, He allows the sun to shine in our lives as well. The warmth and beauty of a sun-filled day lifts our spirits and fills us with joy. We will enjoy even greater SONshine in heaven. The glory of the Lord will be so great that there is no need for the sun or moon! The glory of God! We can get a glimmer of the SONshine here on earth if we allow Jesus to shine in us.

Lord, let Jesus be the light the light that shines in my life; I want to let the SON shine in.

September 20
LIVING DEAD

"He who has the Son has life; he who does not have the Son of God does not have life."

1 John 5:12

Jesus makes life worth living. Unfortunately, too many people are walking around dead. Spiritually dead, emotionally dead, socially dead, and morally dead. When we find our Christian lives on life support there are some things we can do about it. An article on Crosswalk.com but Carrie Courane recommends scheduled time with God; go to church; get involved in church; join a Bible study; join a small group; pray about everything; listen to worship and praise music, and join an online Christian group. All of these will help raise the dead places in our lives. No more living dead; we have been made alive in Christ. We have life in Christ.

Lord, thank you for the life we have been given through Christ.

September 21
NO LOVE NO GOD,
KNOW LOVE KNOW GOD

"He who does not love does not know God, for God is love."
1 John 4:8

Praise Him, praise Him, all you little children. God is love, God is love. Praise Him, praise Him, all you little children. God is love, God is love." The very first Bible verse I memorized as a child was "God is love." I can recall repeating the verse over and over again with my parents until I had committed it to memory. Then it became more than something that was in my head, it was written in my heart. We may not always feel like God loves us, but we can be assured that God loves us for God IS love. Therefore, if we know love, we know God. But if we do not know love, we do not know God.

Lord, let me know love so that I may know you.

September 22
JOY-FULL

"And these things we write to you that your joy may be full."

1 John 1:4

There is a difference in happiness and joy. Happiness is based on feelings and feelings are fickle. Happiness is based on circumstance. Joy is based on our relationship with Christ. Circumstance does not determine our joy. Our joy comes from being in right relationship with Christ. We develop our relationship with Christ by reading and studying the Word of God on a regular basis. The word of God fills us with joy. It gives us joy in sorrow and hope for tomorrow. There is an importance of studying God's word. In order for our joy to be full we must be diligent in studying God's word. Be joy-full.

Lord, thank you for the joy that you give to our relationship in Christ.

September 23
GIVE

"Give and it will be given to you: good measure, pressed down, shaken together, and running over will be put into your boson. For with the same measure that you use, it will be measured back to you."

Luke 6:38

Many times, we are reluctant to share with others what we have been blessed with. In the scripture above, we admonished not to be stingy when we give to others. God promises that we will receive with the same measure we gave. It may not always come back in the same form, but this scripture lets us know that it will be given back to us! Isn't it good to know that there are benefits to having a giving heart?

Lord, help me to give freely from my heart as you lead me to.

September 24

GIVE IT TO GOD

"casting all your cares [all your anxieties, all your worries, and all your concerns, once and for all] on Him, for He cares about you [with deepest affection, and watches over you very carefully]."

1 Peter 5:7 (AMP)

The story has been told about the little girl who took her broken toy to her father and asked him to fix. She waited and waited, but then burst into tears that her father never fixed her toy. Her father lovingly replied that she brought the toy to him, but never let go of the toy so that he could fix it. How many times have we done the same thing to God? We bring our cares, worries, and concerns to God, but we never take our hands off the situation so that God can fix it. What makes you anxious? What keeps you awake with worry? Which concerns cause you to cry? We have been instructed to take all our cares, our anxieties, worries, and concerns to the Lord and leave them there. We can trust God to handle it. Why? Because He cares for us.

Lord, let us give all of our cares over to you because you care for us.

September 25
COVERED BY LOVE

"Above all, love each other deeply, because love covers over a multitude of sins."

1 Peter 4:8 (NIV)

Louis Zamperini was an Olympic runner and World War II officer who survived a horrific plane crash, a seven-week journey across the Pacific in a raft, near starvation and unspeakable torture in Japanese POW camps. Zamperini returned in 1998 to Japan where he was held captive to reunite with his captor and bring him the message of salvation through Jesus Christ. He wanted particularly to forgive his primary tormentor but he refused to meet with him. Zamperini wanted to share the transformative love of Christ with his former tormentor. Love is essential to salvation. Salvation is based on God's love for us and our love for Him. Love shapes us into the very character of Christ. It shapes our speech, affects our actions, and gives meaning to our motivations. When we love one another deeply we cover one another with love.

Lord, help me to love other people deeply so that love can cover any wrongdoings and make forgiveness easier.

September 26
SAVIOR AND LORD

"Honor Christ and let him be the Lord of your life."

1 Peter 3:15a (CEV)

I love to play the board game Monopoly. I especially like to be the banker who collects and distributes money from the bank. The banker was also the one who holds the "get out of jail free" card. This is the card that allows you to skip going to jail. Many Christians expect a similar experience with salvation. They view salvation as a "get out of hell free" card or "fire" insurance. They don't want to go to hell, but they don't want to come under the Lordship of Christ. As a preacher once said during revival, "They want Christ as Savior but not as Lord. They want His blessings, but they don't want correction. They want opportunities, but they don't want to obey. They want things from Him, but they don't want to wait on Him." They want salvation from eternal damnation, but they do not want Lordship over their lives. When Christ is Lord of our lives, we read the word, we pray all the time and about everything, and we grow more and more like Christ.

Lord, help me every day to embrace you as Savior and Lord of my life and let you be Savior and Lord.

September 27
WHO I AM

"But you are a chosen generation, a royal priesthood, a holy nation, His own special people, that you may proclaim the praises of Him who called you out of darkness into His marvelous light;"
1 Peter 2:9

Knowledge is power. The more you know, the more you grow. ASK, always seek knowledge. Knowledge of self is essential. Self-esteem is something even Christian women struggle with. The world is constantly telling us who we are or who we should be. We see ourselves in light of the world's standards. Am I pretty enough? Am I smart enough? Am I thin enough? All the superficial definitions of self. Our true identity is found only in Christ. In Him we are a chosen generation, a royal priesthood, a holy nation, and His own special people.

Lord, remind me daily who and whose I am, not who others say that I am.

September 28
BROKEN BUT BEAUTIFUL

"He has made everything beautiful in its time."

Ecclesiastes 3:11a

We can face ugly situations in life. One of the ugliest is the death of a parent. When my mom was diagnosed with cancer, it was an ugly day. When my mom breathed her last breath in the hospital bed it was a broken day. When my mom died my world shattered into a million pieces. But when I thought about my mom being in the presence of the Lord with no more cancer, no more pain—the broken day became beautiful. We serve a God that has made EVERYTHING beautiful in its time. The ugly in life He makes beautiful. The pain in life, He makes beautiful. The broken in life, He makes beautiful. He makes everything beautiful in its own time.

Lord, thank you for making the broken, painful, and shattered pieces of my life beautiful.

September 29
SHALLOW

"Those on the rocky soil are the people who, when they hear, receive and welcome the word with joy; but these have no firmly grounded root. They believe for a while, and in time of trial and temptation they fall away [from Me and abandon their faith]."

Luke 8:13 (AMP)

There is more to Christianity than shouting, joy, and prosperity. God will give us shouting for sorrow, joy for the journey, and prosperity in all areas of life—not just the material. Unfortunately, we lack deep faith. A faith that is rooted and firmly grounded. We receive and welcome the gospel as long as it benefits us—this is shallow. However, when trials, trouble, and temptation come, we fall away rather than cling to our faith. As seasoned saints, trials should serve as opportunities to draw closer to God and cling to our faith.

Lord, let trials and temptations lead me to you and grow my faith.

September 30
TOO WEAK TO PRAY

"In the same way the Spirit also joins to help in our weakness, because we do not know what to pray for as we should, but the Spirit Himself intercedes for us with unspoken groanings."
Romans 8:26 (HCSB)

Have you ever been too weak to pray? There have been three times in my life that my spirit and flesh felt too weak to pray. I felt unable to utter words in prayer: when my mom died, when I had a miscarriage, and before I was finally correctly diagnosed with fibroids. When my mom died I was hurt and couldn't pray. When my child passed I was grieving and couldn't pray. When I was sick and couldn't get well, I was frustrated and couldn't pray. I was emotionally, spiritually, and physically unable to pray. The words would not form on my lips, but they formed on my heart and rolled from my eyes down my cheeks. In times like these, how wonderful it is to know that we have an intercessor. When we are weak and don't know what to pray, the Holy Spirit intercedes on our behalf.

Lord, when I am weak and don't know what or how to pray, thank you for sending the Intercessor on my behalf.

OCTOBER

October 1
FINDING GRACE

"Let us therefore come boldly to the throne of grace, that we may obtain mercy and find grace to help in time of need."
Hebrews 4:16

When we are in trouble, we seek help. As Christians, we seek God in prayer. In prayer, we find grace and obtain mercy. Grace. God's unmerited favor. Grace. Getting what we do not deserve. Grace. Help in the time of need. Grace. We can come to God boldly. Grace. Trusting that He will give us exactly what we need, when we need it. Grace. The unlimited resources of God applied to our situation. Mercy. God's love when I don't want it. Mercy. Not getting what I deserve. When we go to God in prayer, we will find grace and obtain mercy, exactly what we need.

Lord, when I am in need let me seek you to find grace and obtain mercy, both are exactly what I need.

October 2
MAKE A FOOL OUT YOURSELF

"For we too once were foolish, disobedient, deceived, enslaved to various sinful desires and pleasures, spending and wasting our life in malice and envy, hateful, hating one another."

Titus 3:3 (AMP)

When I was in college, my friends and I loved to dance. It wouldn't matter if no one else were dancing, we would. I recall one song had a refrain that said, "make a fool out yourself!" How many times have we done that in our lives? Our lives without Christ in control are foolish, disobedient, self-serving. Instead of God chasing, we're pleasure seeking. We fail to treasure moments and instead waste time on malice, envy, and hate. Basically, without Christ, we make a fool out of ourselves.

Lord, don't let me forget that without you I am making a fool of myself.

October 3
DON'T GO THERE

"Run from temptations that capture young people. Always do the right thing. Be faithful, loving, and easy to get along with. Worship with people whose hearts are pure. Stay away from stupid and senseless arguments. These only lead to trouble,"
2 Timothy 2:22-23 (CEV)

One of my favorite movies of all times is *Forest Gump*. All though there are several memorable scenes, one of my favorites is little Jenny yelling, "Run, Forrest! Run!" As Christians, there are some things we should just avoid. But it isn't enough to simply avoid temptation, we must run from temptation to something better. We should run from temptation toward doing right, toward being faithful, toward being loving, and toward fellowshipping with like-minded people. When temptation arises, and it will, we should hear "Run, Christian! Run!" in our ears.

Lord, I will run from temptation and run toward right living.

October 4

FIGHT

"We have to fight to keep our faith. Try as hard as you can to win that fight. Take hold of eternal life. It is the life you were chosen to have when you confessed your faith in Jesus—that wonderful truth that you spoke so openly and that so many people heard."

1 Timothy 6:12 (ERV)

Layla Ali is the daughter of the Muhamad Ali, the greatest boxer of all times. She was a premiere fighter in her career; she retired from her boxing career. She retired from her boxing career with a 24-0 boxing record. She fought to win. As Christians, we are in a fight. We must fight to keep our faith. Daily, sometimes minute by minute, our opponent jabs at us at home, at work, at church, and socially. We must constantly stick and move. When we fail to do that we will fall to fear. Fear is not of God. We must; we have to fight to keep the faith.

Lord, let me fight the good fight of faith so that I may win.

October 5
WE ARE FAMILY

"Don't speak angrily to an older man. But talk to him as if he were your father. Treat the younger men like brothers. Treat the older women like mothers. And treat the younger women with respect like sisters."

1 Timothy 5:1-2 (ERV)

Being raised in the South, respect, and manners are the standard. "Yes ma'am, no ma'am." "Yes sir, no sir." "Hey sis, hey bro." All of these are common everyday greetings. Our elders have warned us to mind how we treat people. They were advising us from the Bible. In first Timothy, we are advised on how to treat elders and youngers. Older men as fathers, younger men as brothers, older women as mothers, younger women as sisters. In the body of Christ, we are all family. We should treat one another as such.

Lord, let me always mind how I treat other people.

October 6
STAY IN YOUR LANE

"and to make it your ambition to lead a quiet life: You should mind your own business and work with your hands, just as we told you,"

1 Thessalonians 4:11 (NIV)

When I was learning to drive, I tended to drift into the other lanes. It took practice and a few yells from well-meaning parents to get the feel of staying in my lane. Similarly, in our Christian walk it is easy to drift into areas that we should not be in. The Bible advises us to lead quiet lives and mind our own business. In a world full of real-life drama and reality TV, it is more essential than ever for us to stay in our lane. Drama in life, on tv, and online is often the result of people being loud, not minding their own business, and not focusing on their own lives. If only we would live quietly and mind our own business.

Lord, let me strive to stay in my lane, live quietly, and mind my business.

October 7
ROOTED IN TRUTH

"You have accepted Christ Jesus as your Lord. Now keep on following him. Plant your roots in Christ and let him be the foundation for your life. Be strong in your faith, just as you were taught. And be grateful. Don't let anyone fool you by using senseless arguments. These arguments may sound wise, but they are only human teachings. They come from the powers of this world[a] and not from Christ."

Colossians 2:6-8 (CEV)

Roots are essential to plant growth and development. Roots serve three primary functions: absorbing essential nutrients from the soil, helping to anchor the plant so that it does not fall, and helping store extra nutrients for future use. As Christians, our roots should be in Christ for the same three reasons. In Christ, we absorb the essential characteristics and elements to live an abundant life. In Christ, we are anchored to the Solid Rock so that we are not tossed to and from by every wind and doctrine. Finally, in Christ, we have promises that are not just for future use but are eternal.

Lord, let me be rooted in Christ for spiritual nourishment, a firm foundation, and eternal promises.

October 8
SATISFIED WITH JESUS

"I am telling you this, but not because I need something. I have learned to be satisfied with what I have and with whatever happens. I know how to live when I am poor and when I have plenty. I have learned the secret of how to live through any kind of situation—when I have enough to eat or when I am hungry, when I have everything I need or when I have nothing."

Philippians 4:11-12 (ERV)

One of my favorite old hymns of the church is "Satisfied with Jesus." The lyrics say, "I'm satisfied with Jesus, satisfied with Jesus, satisfied with Jesus in my heart. I'm satisfied with Jesus, satisfied with Jesus, satisfied with Jesus in my heart." It then goes on to other verses saying, "You can't make me doubt him. I know too much about Him. Thank you, thank you, Jesus." It is the last verse, thanking Jesus that expresses the gratitude that should reside with Christians. Not only that, in a world that constantly tells us how dissatisfied we are, we must learn to be content. We should learn to be satisfied with what we have and whatever happens. I'm satisfied with Jesus.

Lord, let me be content with what I have and always remembering that what I have comes from you.

October 9
BE FRUIT-FULL

"The Holy Spirit produces a different kind of fruit: unconditional love, joy, peace, patience, kindheartedness, goodness, faithfulness,"

Galatians 5:22 (VOICE)

The Bible tells us that a person is known by the fruit they bear. If we are in the world, our flesh will produce fruit that includes hate, pain, worry, impatience, meanness, badness, and disloyalty. These should not be character traits of Christians. We should be fruit-full with the fruit of the Spirit. These include love, joy, peace, patience, kindheartedness, goodness, and faithfulness. These are the characteristics that identify a fruit-full Christian life. If we work to bear these fruit in our daily lives, we will grow daily in the Character of Christ.

Lord, let me bear the fruit of the Spirit in my life: love, joy, peace, patience, kindheartedness, goodness, and faithfulness.

October 10
MAKE A CHOICE

"But maybe you don't want to serve the Lord. You must choose for yourselves today. Today you must decide who you will serve. Will you serve the gods that your ancestors worshiped when they lived on the other side of the Euphrates River? Or will you serve the gods of the Amorites who lived in this land? You must choose for yourselves. But as for me and my family, we will serve the Lord."

Joshua 24:15 (ERV)

Life is full of choices, from what to wear, what to eat, what to do. There are other choices we have to make daily in order to reflect the character of Christ. Should I share this post? Should I tweet this thought? Is this post one I should share on Instagram? Each choice bears its consequences. The most important choice we make is to choose Christ. Once we choose Him as our Lord and Savior; we must then daily choose the things of God.

Lord, let me always choose you and your ways in my life.

311

October 11
LIKE MINDED
"Adopt the attitude that was in Christ Jesus:"
Philippians 2:5 (CEB)

Let this mind be in you that was in Jesus…but how? How do I take on the mind of Christ? READ the word. Jesus studied the scriptures often, that is how He was able to quote it and stand on it. We can't be what we've never seen. We can't say what we've never heard. We can't remember what we've never read. PRAY (praise repent ask yield) to God, often. Prayer, for baby believers, can be nothing more than childhood memorizations, vain repetitions, and selfish requests. Prayer for seasoned saints is an ongoing conversation with God. GROW in the character of Christ. We should daily seek to grow in the grace and knowledge of God regularly. We adopt the attitude of Christ Jesus when we READ, PRAY, and GROW.

Lord, let me seek opportunities daily to READ Your Word, PRAY to you, and GROW in the grace and knowledge of God daily.

October 12
WANT WHAT GOD WILLS

"Take delight in the Lord, and he will give you your heart's desires. Commit everything you do to the Lord. Trust him, and he will help you."

Psalm 37:4-5 (NLT)

Security sells in a world of threats and uncertainty. In fact, the advertising slogans play on our desire to be safe. "You're in good hands." "Like a good neighbor." "Always there." The safest place in the whole world is in the center of the will of God. But how do I know that I am in His will? His will can be found in His word. If what I am doing, or thinking, or saying cannot be found in His word, then it is not His will. Next, we should delight ourselves in the Lord. When we do this, we take on the heart of Christ and our heart turns to the things that touch the heart of God. Then our heart will desire the things of God. Finally, we should commit everything we do to the Lord trusting Him and He will help us.

Lord, let me want what you will so that I delight in you, commit everything to you and trust you.

October 13
LOVE DOESN'T HURT

"But speaking the truth in love, let us grow in every way into Him who is the head—Christ."

Ephesians 4:15 (HCSB)

Children tell the truth whether we want to hear it or not. "You look fat." "You stink." "You're not telling the truth." "You're mean." The honesty of children is innocent and refreshing. It comes from a place of love and caring. They truly speak the truth in love. As we grow older, we shy away from the truth. We know that people are hurting, in need, need encouragement, or are in pain and yet we do nothing. Let us grow in Christ by speaking the truth in love.

Lord, let me speak the truth in love daily so that I can grow into the character of Christ.

October 14
IN THE HOUSE

"Therefore you are no longer outsiders (exiles, migrants, and aliens, excluded from the rights of citizens), but you now share citizenship with the saints (God's own people, consecrated and set apart for Himself); and you belong to God's [own] household."
Ephesians 2:19 (AMPC)

I am an only child, the only lonely of my parents. My husband, on the other hand, has an identical twin brother and several other siblings. One thing I have observed with my husband and his siblings is that they may argue, fuss and fight, but at the end of the day it is all love. Why? They are family. They are blood. They belong to the same household. Our feelings are fickle and can't be fully trusted. But if we allow the Holy Spirit to lead and direct our actions, we will relate to those in the household of faith, even our immediate family, in a more loving manner. We were once outsiders but now we are a part of the family of God. We should act as though we are all in the house.

Lord, let me treat all the members of the household of faith with love and respect.

October 15
WARRIOR CHRISTIANS

"For though we live in the body, we do not wage war in an unspiritual way, since the weapons of our warfare are not worldly, but are powerful through God for the demolition of strongholds. We demolish arguments and every high-minded thing that is raised up against the knowledge of God, taking every thought captive to obey Christ. And we are ready to punish any disobedience, once your obedience has been confirmed."
2 Corinthians 10:3-6 (HCSB)

Love may be a battlefield but the Christian walk is all out war! Daily we go to battle in our homes, on our jobs, in the gym, at church—everywhere. To be successful in war, you must have the proper weapons. The weapons of our warfare are not of this world but powerful through God. The weapons in our arsenal include truth, righteousness, peace, faith, salvation, Word of God, and prayer (Ephesians 6:10-18). We need to know what we are fighting against and what we are fighting for. We are fighting against strongholds, arguments, and disobedience. We are fighting for our family and our friends. We are warriors, fighting a spiritual warfare.

Lord, let me be a warrior who uses the spiritual warfare you have equipped me with.

October 16
RESTORING RELATIONSHIPS

"so that, on the contrary, you ought rather to forgive and comfort him, lest perhaps such a one be swallowed up with too much sorrow. Therefore I urge you to reaffirm your love to him."

2 Corinthians 2:7-8

Hurt people, hurt people. Everybody hurts sometimes. Unfortunately, the world gives the green light to hurt others when we are hurting. Even as Christians, we tend to be more vulnerable to hurt others when we are hurting. At home, at work, at church, we hurt people and people hurt us each day. The Bible provides guidance on how we can get past the hurt and restore relationships. Restoration is a three-step process: forgive, comfort, and reaffirm love. Forgive the person for what was said or done. Comfort the person by understanding how they are also feeling. Reaffirm your love for them, despite the dispute. This is how we restore our relationships as Christians.

Lord, do not let me allow disputes to separate relationships. Let me always restore relationships by forgiving, comforting, and reaffirming my love.

October 17
I'M STILL STANDING

"Be watchful, stand firm in the faith, act like men, be strong."
1 Corinthians 16:13 (ESV

I have a beautiful art print in my cube that says, "Push yourself higher than your heels." Every time I glance at that print throughout my workday I sit up a little straighter, I focus more purposely, and I work a little harder. As a professional woman in a STEM field, there is a lot of professional pressure to fail. In order to stand tall, we must have God within. One of the primary ways to have God within is to read and study His word. When we know the word of God, we can stand firm on his promises. It is a firm foundation and I'm still standing. Now for my ladies reading this book, this scripture doesn't mean that you need to literally act as men. Paul is just reminding us to be strong in the face of trials. Trials and tribulations are sure to come our way regardless of our gender! The only way we can brace ourselves for the attack is to stand firm in our faith, read and apply the Word of God, and pray without ceasing.

Lord, in you, I can be watchful, stand firm, and be strong.

October 18
YOU KNOW LORD
"God, you know every sin I've committed; My life's a wide-open book before you."

Psalm 69:5 (MSG)

When I was five or six, I was up one-morning watching cartoons and eating cereal. There was a stubborn piece of hair that kept falling in my eye, so I did what any five or six year old would do. I took a pair of scissors and cut it off. I instantly realized that I had made the wrong decision. Growing fearful of the consequences of my actions, I attempted to hide the evidence of my actions under the couch. Mommy would never be the wiser, right? Wrong. Not only did mommy find the missing patch of hair when she combed my hair later that morning, but I also lied and told her I had thrown the hair away. The missing hair was later discovered under the couch when mommy was vacuuming. By that time, the consequences for my actions had doubled because I had not only cut my hair, but I also lied to my mommy hoping she wouldn't know—mommy knows! Why do we act as if God cannot see our sin? God made us and knows us. He knows every sin we have committed. Those things we did that we should not have done. Those things we failed to do that we should have done. The thoughts we should not have thought. Every sinful thought, word, or deed—He knows. The good news is that He knows, but He still loves us anyway! Thank God you know!

Lord, forgive me for my sins of omission, commission; for every thought or deed, all the things you already know.

October 19
REVIVAL

"Will you not revive us again, that Your people may rejoice in You?"

Psalm 85:6

The Great Awakening in the American Colonies occurred in the 1730s. Concern was raised that colonists were far too concerned with worldly matters especially accumulating wealth. Awakening preachers preached with fury, conviction, and emotion that drew people to them. The message was one of repentance, love, and equality. Revival had come. Revival begins with us. It is more than an annual summer occurrence at our churches. Revival is needed whenever our souls need renewal. Revival revives us to repent. Revival makes us more loving. Revival moves us to justice and equality.

Lord, send a revival and let it begin with me.

October 20
FAIL FORWARD

"My flesh and my heart fail; But God is the strength of my heart and my portion forever."

Psalm 73:26

Failure should be our teacher, not our undertaker. Failure is delay, not defeat. It is a temporary detour, not a dead end. Failure is something we can avoid only by saying nothing, doing nothing, and being nothing." - Denis Waitley. Failure is not optional in life. It is an assurance. At some time in our lives we will all fail. However, it is our reaction to failure that makes all the difference. As Christians, we should fail forward. Every defeat had us down, but not out. Every time we thought we lost, we actually gained. We should find opportunity in the obstacle of failure. The Bible tells us that our flesh will fail, but God is the strength of our heart.

Lord, whenever I fail, let me fail forward turning obstacles into opportunities to try again.

October 21
DELAYED BUT NOT DENIED

"Now Jesus loved Martha and her sister and Lazarus. So, when He heard that he was sick, He stayed two more days in the place where He was."

John 11:5-6

Neither rain, nor snow, nor decades passed can stop the United States Post Office from delivering the mail. One woman received not one, but three letters originally sent in 1969 in 2014! Even though the delivery of the letters was severely delayed, the joy they brought with them could not be denied. Delay does not mean denied. We must come to accept that our timing is not God's timing. God is not constrained by time. He works in and out of time. There are two things we can be sure of and that is Jesus loves us and He will show up. It is not a question of does Jesus love us or if he will show up. He does and He will.

Lord, remind me that when your answer is delayed, it does not mean that it is denied.

October 22
BUT GOD

"You planned evil against me; God planned it for good to bring about the present result—the survival of many people"

Genesis 50:20 (HCSB)

ut God: Changes Everything" by Herbert Cooper describes the moments in life when God comes in and alters our paths. It could also be described as a "divine interruption." Like Cooper, we all have had God to step into the midst of our sinful lives and alter our paths with a divine interruption. The phrase "but God" is one of the most meaningful phrases in the entire Bible. It reminds us that God intervenes on behalf of His people, preparing divine interruptions throughout our life's journey.

Lord, whatever was meant for evil, cause a divine interruption for my good.

October 23
ASK

"Now if any of you lacks wisdom, he should ask God, who gives to all generously and without criticizing, and it will be given to him. But let him ask in faith without doubting. For the doubter is like the surging sea, driven and tossed by the wind."

James 1:5-6 (HCSB)

I teach an introduction to geography course at our local community college. For the last few years, my students have taken a geographic literacy quiz given by National Geographic to young adults age 18-24. My students' results lined up with the results of their peers. They clearly lack geographic wisdom prior to taking my course:

- 37% of young Americans cannot locate Iraq on a map
- 6 out of 10 do not speak another language fluently
- 48% believe the majority population in India is Muslim (it is actually Hindu)
- ½ cannot find New York on a map

The key to wisdom is asking for it. ASK—always seek knowledge. If we desire to be wise, we should ask God to give us wisdom. Not only that we should ask without doubting. When we ask, we ask believing knowing that God will do it, if we ASK.

Lord, if I ask, let me receive your wisdom.

October 24
UNLIMITED POWER

"God's power is unlimited. He needs no teachers"

Job 36:22 (CEV)

I am an environmental scientist by profession. One area that I am starting to learn more and more about is energy. In the United States, our power is generated primarily from coal 38.7%, gas 27.5%, oil 0.7%, nuclear 19.5%, hydro 6.2%, and non-hydro renewables. Although our primary power source is coal, there are other sources as well, including renewable energy, whose usage is growing by leaps and bounds. In the United States, no power source is unlimited. All power is conditional. This is true in our own lives as well. Though we may each exert a certain amount of power in certain areas of our lives, our power is limited. While our power is limited, our God is omnipotent, all-powerful. No matter what situation we face in life, God's power is greater than our problems. While our power is limited, God's power is unlimited.

Lord, your power is unlimited and I can rest in that no matter what problems come my way.

October 25
WORK IN PROGRESS

"God is the one who began this good work in you, and I am certain that he won't stop before it is complete on the day that Christ Jesus returns."

Philippians 1:6 (CEV)

Mount Rushmore took 14 years to carve. The carving took place between October 4, 1927, and October 31, 1941. It was created by Guton Borglum and 400 workers. There were no fatalities during all the carving. The work conditions varied from the blazing heat of summer to bitter cold and windy winter. Ninety percent of the project was done with dynamite. In our children's choir we sang a song entitled, "He Who Began a Good Work in You." I also recall a sign in my Sunday School class that said, "I know I'm somebody 'cause God don't make no junk." One of the old refrains of the church is "I am not what I should be, but thanks be to God; I am not what I used to be!" I am a living testimony. I should have been dead and gone, but Lord you let me live on. Christianity is a journey, not a destination. From the moment of salvation, God begins a good work in us and works it until it is finally complete on the day of glorification. In the meantime, we are all works in progress.

Lord, I am a work in progress, please complete the work that you have begun in my life.

October 26
THE REAL CODE

"Knowing the correct password—saying 'Master, Master,' for instance—isn't going to get you anywhere with me. What is required is serious obedience—doing what my Father wills."

Matthew 7:21 (MSG)

Anyone who has spent any time near a church at all is familiar with "church talk." Those sayings and phrases we frequently use, but cannot be found anywhere in the Bible. "This too shall pass." "God helps those who help themselves." "Spare the rod, spoil the child." "Money is the root of all evil." "Cleanliness is next to godliness." "The Lord works in mysterious ways." "The devil made me do it." What is required of Christians is "serious obedience." As we grow in Christ, we should be more aware of what the Word of God actually says. When you know better, you do better. Knowing "church talk" or other passwords doesn't make us Christians.

Lord, let me practice serious obedience by wanting what you will in my life.

October 27
HE IS

"I gave up all that inferior stuff so I could know Christ personally, experience his resurrection power, be a partner in his suffering, and go all the way with him to death itself."

Philippians 3:10

We have a young adult prayer group at church and we often pose questions to one another regarding our walk with the Lord. I asked my Prayer Friends who God was to them and I was overwhelmed by the responses. Similarly to the Vivian Green song "He Is," they proceeded to rattle off a list of who God is to them. He is Savior, Lord, Healer, Provider, Everything, All Mighty, Keeper, Daddy, All and All, Lord, and My Hiding Place. As Christians, we have given up everything that is inferior to have a real and intimate relationship with Christ. What we call God is directly related to how we know and have experienced God. That says who He is.

Lord, I want to know you intimately so that I can be close to you.

October 28
HE ALWAYS ANSWERS

"So we fasted and entreated our God for this, and He answered our prayer."

Ezra 8:23

We had a great lesson on the "Power and Practice of Prayer: Does God Always Answer Prayer?" The lesson described four different ways God answers: "I can't hear you," "No, " "Yes," or "Wait." If there is sin in our lives, God can't hear us. Sins we haven't repented of hinder our prayers. Sometimes the answer is "no," but like loving parents, the "no" is always in our best interest. God also says "yes" to our requests if they are in His will. Sometimes we must be patient and wait on God's timing. Delay does not mean denied. No matter what God says, He always answers our prayers.

Lord, thank you for always hearing and answering my prayers.

October 29
WITH LOVE

"Let all that you do be done with love."

1 Corinthians 16:14

I am very sentimental and nostalgic. I still hand write letters and cards to my friends and family (my framily). I also enjoy printing my digital photos and sending the captured moments to my framily. If I am feeling exceptionally loving, I will place one of the printed digital pictures inside of the card. I believe in capturing memories and being able to return to those moments over and over again. Unlike a text that can be deleted, letters, cards, and photographs can be kept for a lifetime. Today, sending letters and cards, as well as printing pictures is rare. My framily feels special whenever they receive something from me in the mail. The loving intent is easily identified. It should be the same with our Christian walk. What our world needs now more than ever is love. Imagine if everything we did we did in love.

Lord, let everything that I do be done with love.

October 30
BECAUSE I CAN, DOESN'T MEAN I SHOULD

"We are allowed to do anything, but not everything is good for us to do. We are allowed to do anything, but not all things help us grow strong as Christians."

1 Corinthians 10:23 (NLV)

I couldn't wait to turn ten so I could get my first relaxer. I couldn't wait to turn thirteen to become a teenager. Sixteen, I could drive and wear makeup. Eighteen, leave for college. Twenty-one, order my first glass of wine. Twenty-five, have my car insurance drop. Just because we can do anything, doesn't mean we should do anything. Everything we do, everything we say should bring God glory. It should also edify others. I'm free to wear makeup, but my appearance should be modest. We are free to drink wine, but should not be drunk. We should enjoy the company of the opposite sex, but stay virtuous. Just because we can do whatever we want to do, doesn't me we should do everything.

Lord, do not let me take advantage of my freedom in Christ and do not allow me to cause another Christian to stumble in their walk.

October 31
RUN TO WIN

"You know that only one person gets a crown for being in a race even if many people run. You must run so you will win the crown."

1 Corinthians 9:24 (NLV)

I ran track in high school my freshman year. I even qualified for the Girl's State competition in the 4 x 100m and 4 x 400m relays. I also ran in the meet in the individual 100m and 200m sprints. There are some track fundamentals that are essential to completing a race. First, line up on but not over the start line. Next, secure your feet in the starting blocks. Don't jump the gun, wait for it. Finally, stay in your lane, finish the race and run to win. These fundamentals also apply to the Christian race. The starting line is salvation. Once we are saved, we should set our feet on the building blocks of the Word of God. Next, we shouldn't jump the gun on what God would have us to do and wait on Him. We need to stay in our lane for what God has called us to do. Finally, run to win.

Lord, let me run the race, stay in my lane, and run to win.

NOVEMBER

November 1
EXIT HERE

"No temptation has overtaken you except such as is common to man; but God is faithful, who will not allow you to be tempted beyond what you are able, but with the temptation will also make the way of escape, that you may be able to bear it."

1 Corinthians 10:13

My friend and I were traveling out of town together and came upon a wreck on the interstate right outside of our destination. At the last minute, we exited off hoping to bypass the accident. Sure enough, the accident occurred directly beneath the overpass and we were able to exit off the interstate and bypass the accident. In life, we are often tempted. However, we do not have to be overtaken by temptation. We will not be tempted beyond what we are able. In the time of trouble, God always provides an exit. A way of escape is available if we only exit here.

Lord, let me always look to you in the time of temptation to provide a way of escape.

November 2
IT'S ALL GOD

*"Who says that you are better than anyone else? What do you
have that you didn't receive? And if you received it, then why are
you bragging as if you didn't receive it?"*

1 Corinthians 4:7 (CEB)

There was a popular saying when I was in high school, "It's all good." Though some of my peers continue to use this 1990's slang, lol, I have grown to say, "It's all God." Another one of my favorite sayings is, "Won't He do it?" My friends will respond, "Yes, He will!" Everything that we have comes from God. We are foolish to think otherwise. God has given us everything. We should, therefore, give all credit to Christ and all glory to God.

**Lord, let me never forget that all that I have comes from you;
it's all God.**

November 3
KNOCK OFFS

"But be on your guard, my dear children, against every false god!"

1 John 5:21 (PHILLIPS)

In college, I was introduced to knock-off designer purses. All the benefits of the designer without the cost, or so I thought. Unlike the original, knock-offs are poorly made and full of defects. Try filling up a knock-off purse at your own risk. Similarly, in life we often invest time and effort in people, things, and status—all the while not realizing those are idols. Knock off gods poor made and full of defects. Jimmy Nedham in his song "Clear the Stage" said: "Anything I put before my God is an idol. Anything I want with all my heart is an idol. Anything I can't stop thinking of is an idol. Anything that I give all my love is an idol." Why chase after knock-offs when as Christians we have the real thing?

Lord, let me always remember that I have the real God, I don't need a knock-off.

November 4

PEOPLE WATCH YOU AT MIDNIGHT

"But at midnight Paul and Silas were praying and singing hymns to God, and the prisoners were listening to them."

Acts 16:25

Midnight is the darkest hour. In fact, research has shown that suicides increase after midnight, and peak between 2-3am. Crime rates also increase after midnight. While the world seems to have bad things happen at midnight, God does some of His best work at midnight. Particularly, saving people. Ask Nicodemus and the Philippian jailer. What do we do during the midnights of life? Those times when life is dark, we feel imprisoned and shackle—what do we do? Our response at midnight is important because as Christians others are watching how we react to trouble. Like Paul and Silas, when we are in the midnights of life we should be praying, singing—praising our way through at midnight.

Lord, teach me to sing, pray, and praise at midnight.

November 5
FOLLOW THE LEADER

"The Lord is my shepherd, I lack nothing. He makes me lie down in green pastures, he leads me beside quiet waters, he refreshes my soul. He guides me along the right paths for his name's sake."

Psalm 23:1-3 (NIV)

Young children provide the most beautiful example of complete trust. I have watched my children play "follow the leader." Big sister by two years leads her little brother around the backyard. Shortly after that, the little brother is leading big sister around. There are no question, no reservations. Our children hold tightly to a parent's hand and follow them. They follow their parent's instruction without guessing, and they are quick to seek and find their way back when lost. If only we would completely trust and follow the Lord in the same way. Follow the leader, trust Him to provide. Follow the leader, let Him lead us to rest. Follow the leader, let Him lead to us. Follow the leader; He will guide us along the right paths. Just follow the leader.

Lord, let me follow you without hesitation or reservation.

November 6
DON'T BE A LAZY CHRISTIAN

"Never be lazy, but work hard and serve the Lord enthusiastically."

Romans 12:11 (NLT)

There is nothing worse than a lazy person. Even more so, there is nothing more worse than a lazy Christian. As Christians, we should be the first to put our best foot forward. As believers, we know that everything we do for God counts! For this reason, we should strive to put our all into everything that we do for God! God doesn't half-step when it comes to us! Today, in everything that you do, strive to do it in excellence. Remember you are working for the Kingdom, not for man! Let your light so shine among men!

Lord, strengthen me to give my all to everything that you have commanded me to do!

LaDonna Michele

November 7

PRAISE IS WHAT I DO

"Praise the Lord, for the Lord is good; sing praises to his name, for that is pleasant!"

Psalm 135:3 (NIV)

On January 20, 2009, America witnessed history as Barack Hussein Obama was inaugurated the 44th President of the United States of America. He was the first African American to hold the office. The event was the largest in attendance of any event in the history of Washington, D.C., the largest attendance of any Presidential Inauguration in United States history, and also the highest online viewership ever of the swearing-in ceremonies. That's a lot of praise for such a momentous and historic occasion. Praise. Webster defines praise as, "the expression of respect and gratitude as an act of worship." The 2009 inauguration was nothing compared to the praise we owe our God. To praise God is to give Him all the glory, honor, thanks, worship, adoration, reverence, exaltation, and devotion. Praise is what we do because He deserves it.

Lord, you are worthy of all the glory, all the honor, and all the praise. I will praise you.

November 8
LESS OF ME

"He must increase, but I must decrease."

John 3:30

Lent occurs from Ash Wednesday (the day after Fat Tuesday) and continues through Good Friday (the Friday before Resurrection Sunday). It is a period of reflection, a time of repentance, and season of change. One main focus is fasting. The Bible tells us that some things will only happen if we pray and fast. Fasting is a way of decreasing or suppressing the desires of our flesh so that the heart and desire for Christ can shine through. Just as John emphasized centuries ago, Christ "must increase, but I must decrease." How do we allow Christ to increase in our lives? First through salvation, allowing Christ to be our Savior and Lord. Next, by reading, studying and applying the word of God in our lives. Regularly attending worship service, bible study, and participating in ministry at a local church. Christ increases when we regularly talk to Him in prayer. Finally, Christ increases when we seek to glorify God in all that we do. These are some basic ways that Christ can increase as we decrease.

Lord, let me decrease and let Christ increase in my life; let there be less of me and more of Christ.

November 9
CHOOSE LIFE

"...I have set before you life and death, blessing and cursing; therefore choose life, that both you and your descendants may live;"

Deuteronomy 30:19b

Huffington Post article cited eleven things we're doing that could shorten our lives. These things included having a hard time finding love, sitting down more than a few hours each day, neglecting our friends, vegging out in front of the TV, etc. Research has also shown that the words we speak can have negative effects on our life expectancy as well. Each day we have choices to make that will either positively or negatively impact our lives. These choices include what we do, but also what we say. Saying the wrong thing can have as serious consequences as doing the wrong thing. In our mouths lie the power of life and death. Let us daily choose to speak life.

Lord, let me always choose life allowing my words and actions to build up, encourage, and motivate myself and others.

November 10
WATCH ME

"Don't let anyone think less of you because you are young. Be an example to all believers in what you say, in the way you live, in your love, your faith, and your purity."

1 Timothy 4:12 (NLT)

My daughter and her friends love to play "Little Sally Walker." The lyrics to the game go, "Little Sally Walker walking down the street, she didn't know what to do so she stopped in front of me and said hey girl do your thing do your thing switch!" It is a fun game of copycat. It is especially funny when a younger player gets an older player to mimic them. Many baby believers think certain behaviors are only for seasoned saints. All saints are to be an example, no matter their age or how long they have been on their faith journey. We must be mindful that someone is always watching us. When they don't know what to do, they watch us and do what we do. Since people are watching us, we need to be an example with our words, our lives, our love, our faith, and our purity.

Lord, let me live a life that is an example to others in words, in love, in faith, and in purity.

November 11
SON RISE

"Very early in the morning, on the first day of the week, they came to the tomb when the sun had risen."

Mark 16:2

Each day, the sun rises in the East and sets in the West. God as the artist decorates the dusk and dawn as a reminder to us that He is author and creator of the universe. As a scientist, I love to observe God in creation. If you ever want to reassure yourself of God being in complete control, look no further than creation, especially sunrise. It reminds me of another "son" rise that occurred. The women had gone to the tomb to anoint the body of Jesus early in the morning. I am sure that their grieving hearts were encouraged by the beauty of the rising sun. Little did they know, they would experience two risings that day. Not only did the sun rise, but the Son had also arisen that day. What great joy they must have felt. We too have the same daily reminder as the sun rises that it is the second rising we have experienced that day. The Son also did rise.

Lord, thank you for letting the sunrise serve as a daily reminder of the Son rise.

MISSION POSSIBLE

*"But Jesus looked at them and said, "With men it is impossible,
but not with God; for with God all things are possible."*

Mark 10:27

Disney's 2004 movie "The Incredibles" is the story of Mr.
Incredible and his family, a group of superheroes forced
into suburban life. Mr. Incredible had super strength and
limited invisibility. His wife, Elastigirl, was able to bend and stretch
her body like elastic. Their daughter Violet was able to turn
invisible and create force shields. Their Son, Dash, had super
speed. The baby son, Jack, was able to shift shapes. The thing
about the Incredibles was that although they possessed
superpowers, their power was limited. People are limited. We are
limited in power. Limited in presence. Limited in control. But not
God. Our God has unlimited power. He has an extensive presence.
With people, some things are possible. With God, all things are
possible.

**Lord, let me always remember that when things are
impossible for me, all things are possible for you.**

347

November 13

CAN YOU HEAR ME NOW

"And this is the confidence that we have toward him, that if we ask anything according to his will he hears us."

1 John 5:13-15 (ESV)

Verizon use to have a commercial where a guy would walk around on his cell phone asking, "Can you hear me now?" Parents experience similar situations on a daily basis. My children have selective hearing. It especially occurs when they are in front of a screen—TV, tablet, or phone. My husband has fallen victim to selective hearing at times as well. We serve a God that always hears our prayers. We can be confident in Christ, that whatever we ask by faith, God hears us. Throughout the Bible, God reminds us that he hears and answers our requests.

Lord, let me remain confident knowing that you hear my prayers.

November 14
REDIRECTED NOT REJECTED

"I will place on his shoulder the key to the house of David; what he opens no one can shut, and what he shuts no one can open."
Isaiah 22:22 (NIV)

History is full of people who were redirected by rejection. Michael Jordan was cut from his high school basketball team. Nelson Mandela spent 27 years in prison before becoming President of South Africa. Oprah Winfrey had a baby at 14 before becoming one of the richest women in America. JK Rowling received 12 rejection letters from publishers before becoming a published author. They are excellent examples of choosing redirection rather than rejection. Most people do not deal with rejection very well. However, as Christians, we should look at every situation in life as an opportunity. We should trust that God is indeed working all things for good. Jesus opens what no one can shut and shuts what no one can open. Sometimes it is not rejection, but redirection.

Lord, may I always remember that every closed door is not rejection, but could be redirection.

November 15
HOLD ON

"Wait on the Lord; Be of good courage, and He shall strengthen your heart; Wait, I say, on the Lord!"

Psalm 27:14

We live in a time where we are obsessed with instant results. We use microwaves more than stoves, text more than call, email more than write letters. Our patience has decreased with increased response time. Waiting is not anything new. Joseph waited 13 years. Abraham waited 25 years. Moses waited 40 years. Jesus waited 30 years. There is a blessing in waiting. There is joy in delayed gratification. While waiting, we can work on what God has already told us to do. While waiting, we can focus on and hope in God's word. While waiting, we can have our courage strengthened. There are blessings in waiting.

Lord, let me wait patiently on you when gratification is delayed.

November 16

EXPECTATION OF TRANSFORMATION

"but be transformed and progressively changed [as you mature spiritually] by the renewing of your mind [focusing on godly values and ethical attitudes],"

Romans 12:2b (AMP)

The life cycle of a frog is an amazing example of transformation. It begins its life as an egg in water. Once it hatches as a tadpole, it is dependent on water to survive. As the tadpole grows, it develops legs, loses its tail and gills, and eventually leaves water for land. The adult frog looks different from the tadpole it began as. If God can do that for a frog, imagine what He can do with us once we are saved. The elders said, "I looked at my hands and they looked new. I looked at my feet and they did too." Tramaine Hawkins said, "A wonderful change has come over me." While Tamela Mann said, "Change Me O God, make me more like you." When we accept Christ we transform. Our very minds are transformed. How do we renew our minds? By reading the Bible daily, praying often, and growing in the character of Christ.

Lord, I expect you to transform me daily and change me into your image.

LaDonna Michele

November 17
SPEAK LIFE

"The tongue has the power of life and death,"

Proverbs 18:21a (NIV)

I learned a valuable lesson in childhood. Sticks and stones may break my bones, but words hurt too. Moving from a diverse military community in Germany to a rural Alabama suburb placed me in uncomfortable situations regarding skin color and accent, or lack thereof. My mom was a stickler for pronunciation and articulation. The words "hee-ouse" and "mee-ouse" were not allowed in my mom's presence. She made it very clear that we are not defined by the color of our skin or our accent. My mother believed in enunciation and pronunciation. She believed in the power of words. Sometimes we defeat ourselves with our mouth. We speak defeat. We speak discouragement. We speak negativity. We speak bad things into our lives and the lives of others. The Bible tells us that the power of life and death is in the tongue.

Lord, let me always choose life and speak life.

November 18
KEEPING IT REAL OR RIGHTEOUS

"Right living was my clothing."

Job 29:14a (ERV)

The Real World New York aired on MTV in 1992 and forever changed TV. It was a unique show at the time. Many people didn't see why anyone would want to watch people as they went about their daily interactions. Twenty-five years later there have been 32 seasons of the Real World, and it is no longer in a category all itself. Reality TV permeates every channel. The refreshing thing about the Real World initially was that the cast was very aware of the presence of the cameras and at least tried to live scandal-free. Not so much with the reality shows today. Our lives are similar to reality TV; we are also constantly under the scrutiny and watch of others. We should, therefore, choose to live right. We spend several hours putting on our physical clothing in the morning, but fail to clothe our spiritual self. We must clothe ourselves in right living.

Lord, let me keep it real by clothing myself daily in right living.

November 19
SOMEHOW AND ANYHOW

"I will clear a way in the desert. I will make rivers on dry land."
Isaiah 43:19b (GW)

Harriet Jacobs was born into slavery. She had a good life as far as slavery goes until the age of 12 when she was sold to a new owner. Her new owner sexually harassed her from the age of 15 until 22. She became pregnant by a caring white man and had two children with him. She finally ran away and hid in the crawl space of her grandparents' home where she could peek at her children below. For seven years she lived in the crawl space about a 9x7 with a low sloping ceiling. The crawl space was infested with rodents, lacked light, and had no ventilation. She finally escaped slavery to freedom in Philadelphia. The Lord had made a way, somehow. It is reassuring that God will make a way not only somehow. In certain situations, God will make a way anyhow. The hymn writer tells us, "The Lord will make a way somehow, when beneath the cross I bow...the Lord will make a way somehow."

Lord, let me never forget that you will make a way somehow and anyhow.

November 20
SELF DISTRACTION

"I am not trying to give you more rules and regulations. I only want to give you advice that is fitting and helpful. I want to help you live lives of faithful devotion to the Lord without any distraction."

1 Corinthians 7:35 (VOICE)

Distracted driving, particularly with cell phones has become a leading cause of car accidents. Statistics have shown that reading one text is equivalent to driving the length of a football field at 55mph without your eyes on the road. 46 states have banned driving and texting. Texting increases the chance of crashing six times. About 56% of parents check phones while driving. And nine people are killed, 1000 injured daily due to distracted driving. We are distracted by our phones and by the enemy. The number one trick of the enemy is distraction. If he can take our focus off of God, he can lead us down a path of distraction to a path of destruction. It is God's will that we live lives devoted to Him and not become distracted.

Lord, do not allow me to be distracted by tricks of the enemy to get my focus off of you.

November 21
DO OVER

"And he answered, 'I will not'; but afterward he regretted it and changed his mind and went."

Matthew 21:29 (AMP)

We get very few opportunities for "do-overs" in life. My grandfather would say there were two things you can never get back, a spoken word and a missed opportunity. We often speak words we regret speaking. We do things we should not have done. When it comes to the things of God, a missed opportunity to be obedient can block or hinder a blessing. There is no gray area. We either obey or disobey. Disobedience in any form is a sin. Delayed obedience is sin. There are blessings in obedience.

Lord, let me always trust and obey.

November 22
STUMBLING BLOCKS
AND STEPPING STONES

"Though they stumble, they will never fall, for the Lord holds them by the hand."

Psalm 37:24 (NLT)

High heels have been linked to leg injuries, knee injuries, and lower back pain. It has also been linked to straining of knees, hips, and backs. Sprains and strains to the ankle or feet are also caused by missteps and stumbles. The way we view trouble makes a major difference in how we handle it when it comes. As Christians, we should view problems as opportunities. My mom would say turn every stumbling block into a stepping stone toward success. My spiritual mentor mama once preached that "a setback, is a setup, for a comeback." The Bible echoes these words by promising that even though we may stumble in life, we won't fall because God holds our hand. God is within us; we will not fall.

Lord, hold my hand and when I stumble, don't let me fall.

357

November 23
DELIGHTFUL DELIVERANCE

"Many are the afflictions of the righteous, but the Lord delivers him out of them all."

Psalm 34:19

Pizza delivery places used to guarantee delivery of a pizza in 30 minutes or less or it was free. In college, we would time the delivery places in hopes of earning a free meal. As believers, we also have a delivery guarantee. The Bible reminds us repeatedly that we will face difficulties in life, but the Lord will deliver us out of every one of them. We can stand on the promise that no matter the difficulty, the distress, or the disease, the Lord will deliver. No matter the circumstance, constraint, or condition, the Lord will deliver. No matter what comes our way, the Lord will deliver.

Lord, when trouble comes and I know it will, let me rest in the assurance that you will deliver me out of them all.

November 24
ANCHORED IN H.O.P.E.

"We have this hope as an anchor for our lives, safe and secure."
Hebrews 6:19a (HCSB)

One of my favorite songs to sing when storms are raging in my life is "My Soul Has Been Anchored In the Lord." The lyrics say, "Though the storms keep on raging in my life And sometimes it's hard to tell the night from day. Still that hope that lies within is reassured. As I keep my eyes upon the distant shore, I know He'll lead me safely to that blessed place He has prepared. But if the storm doesn't cease and if the winds keep on blowing in my life, my soul has been anchored in the Lord." HOPE—having only positive expectations. HOPE—hold on pain ends. HOPE—hang on to positive expectations. HOPE should be the anchor of our lives.

Lord, thank you for the hope that is the anchor for our lives.

November 25
EVERYDAY IS THANKSGIVING

"Give thanks in everything, for this is God's will for you in Christ Jesus."

1 Thessalonians 5:18 (HCSB)

The Friday after Thanksgiving is considered the official start of the Christmas shopping season. Black Friday had been creeping earlier and earlier until it was officially beginning on the evening of Thanksgiving! This was depriving retail workers of their time with family and friends on Thanksgiving. Thankfully, many retailers have gone back to keeping Black Friday on Friday. Thank God! Thankfulness is a lifestyle that must be practiced daily. We learn to thank God for the seemingly little things, when we continuously thank him for the seemingly big things. We must decide to live each day with a thankful heart. Every day is Thanksgiving when you know the Lord.

Lord, give me a thankful heart each day.

November 26
SEASONS

"For everything there is a season, a time for every activity under heaven."

Ecclesiastes 3:1 (NLT)

The writer of Ecclesiastes tells us that there is a time for everything. This should remind us that just as good times don't last always, bad times don't either. In the midst of our trials and tribulations, we can be sure that they won't last long. Instead of focusing on the time, we should focus on the purpose for each season we find ourselves in. Lessons in the hard time teach us how appreciate and handle the good times. In retrospect, the lessons we learn in the good times give us the hope to sustain when the winds of life blow. Regardless of your season, thank God that He is keeping you and protecting you through it all!

Lord, I thank you for every season of life, the good and the bad!

November 27

NO REGRETS

"I have fought the good fight, I have finished the race, I have kept the faith."

2 Timothy 4:7 (HCSB)

I have always had an encouraging spirit. I can remember as young as 2nd and 3rd grade being drawn to those who were hurting. Throughout high school and college, my circle of friends was very diverse with a mix of people of various backgrounds. My joy comes from encouraging others even to my detriment at times. In my late twenties and thirties, I took a spiritual gifts quiz which helped confirm what I already knew in my heart. I am an encourager. My prayer sisters call me "She-Barnabas." Only what we do for Christ will last. So let us continue in the gifts and callings that Christ has given to each one of us. We want to hear well done and have no regrets.

Lord, whatever you have called me to do, let me do it faithfully.

November 28
FROM START TO FINISH

"looking unto Jesus, the author and finisher of our faith,"

Hebrews 12:2a

Our lives begin and end with Jesus. He formed us in our mothers' wombs. He created us in His likeness. He has loved us with an everlasting love. He was thinking about us when we were in sin and not thinking about Him. He drew us with His love. He saved us, forgave us, raised us, and filled us up. He secures our salvation. He uses us to will and to do according to His good pleasure. He is the author and finisher of our faith. So it is Jesus—from start to finish.

Lord, let me always remember that my faith begins and ends with you.

November 29

START RIGHT, KEEP RIGHT

"Each morning you listen to my prayer, as I bring my request to you and wait for your reply."

Psalm 5:3 (CEV)

If your daily life is anything like mine, it is pretty hectic. We rise early, squeeze in a few moments with Jesus, get dressed, wake the kids, and help them get dressed for school. We kiss our spouse goodbye, jump in our car, rush off to work only to be stuck in traffic. We rush to our desk, boot up our computer, and proceed to check emails. If time allows, we shove down our breakfast between emails, teleconferences, meetings, presentations, and phone calls. We take a break during lunch (if we are lucky). Then, it is back to emails, phones, and computers until quitting time. We rush the children to after-school activities and ourselves to meetings. We end the evening with homework, baths for the kids, and time with our spouse before we both fall asleep and then do it all over again in the morning. Whew! With all that is going on expectedly in our daily lives (we won't even speak about the unexpected), it essential that we begin and end each day talking to Jesus. Jesus should be the first person we talk to when our eyes open and the last person when our eyes close. If we start right, we are more likely to stay right.

Lord, let my day begin and end with a little talk with you so that I can start right and stay right.

November 30
SPEAK THE WORD

"For the word of God is living and powerful, and sharper than any two-edged sword, piercing even to the division of soul and spirit, and of joints and marrow, and is a discerner of the thoughts and intents of the heart."

Hebrews 4:12

Would you leave your child or pet in the car all day everyday unsupervised? Or leave them crammed in back window of your car so everyone can see them but are never are taken out? Could you only allow them out of the car once a week? This is exactly how we treat the word of God. It is one of the most underused tools that Christians have at our disposal. When we fail to read and study, we deny its importance and power in our lives. The Bible tells us that the word of God is living and powerful if we would only use it.

Lord, let me daily read, study, and speak your Word.

DECEMBER

December 1
EXAMINE YOURSELF

"Test yourselves to see if you are in the faith. Examine yourselves.
Or do you yourselves not recognize that Jesus Christ is in you?—
unless you fail the test."

2 Corinthians 13:5 (CSB)

One of my favorite things to watch on television are court shows. In fact, I was so caught up in Judge Mathis, Judge Judy, and Judge Joe Brown in high school that I considered pursuing a law degree. I am fascinated by the process of prosecution. The witty questioning seeking to garner information from a witness from cross-examination excites me. The prosecutor hits the witness with a barrage of questions until they're given the information that's needed. In a courtroom drama, we get a glimpse of our spiritual selves. We are told to examine ourselves regularly. As a prosecutor, we are to review the facts of our lives and decide if we are living a Christ-led, Christ-filled, and a Christ-following life. As one writer said, "We cannot call ourselves Christians if our lives are in total denial of what we profess to be." People should not have to wonder or guess if we are Christians. There shouldn't have to be any barrage of questioning to ourselves to discover our Christianity. Our lips and lives should serve as a witness to what we profess to believe. Self-examination should find us guilty of following Christ.

We should regularly examine ourselves and our lives. The elders said, "Search me Lord and if you find anything, not like you, take it out!"

Lord, search me Lord and if you find anything that isn't like you or what it should be, take it out Lord and strengthen me.

December 2

NOT AN OPTION

"Therefore go and make disciples of all nations, baptizing them in the name of the Father and of the Son and of the Holy Spirit, and teaching them to obey everything I have commanded you. And surely I am with you always, to the very end of the age."

Matthew 28:19-20 (NIV)

Failure is not an option when it comes to sharing the "Good News." We have been empowered by the Holy Spirit, commissioned by God, and told by Jesus to share the Good News wherever we go. If we do not do so, we are disobedient. What is witnessing? It is sharing the good news of salvation through Jesus Christ in the power of the Holy Spirit and leaving the results to God. When we do that, we make disciples. The Good News of the Gospel is the power unto salvation. It has the power to transform lives. But most of all, God has commanded us to do it and given us power and ability; therefore failure is not an option.

Lord, send me, use me as your witness to family and friends, those in my community, my state, nation, and the world.

December 3
MARVELOUS AND MIRACULOUS

"The stone which the builders rejected has become the chief cornerstone. This was the Lord's doing; It is marvelous in our eyes. This is the day the Lord has made; We will rejoice and be glad in it."

Psalm 118:22-24

Many people, including children, have lost their sensitivity to the miraculous and marvelous occurrences around us each day. Perhaps because I am an Environmental Scientist, I am a bit more observant of the marvelous and miraculous in my life. When we look in the Bible, there are so many marvelous and miraculous events! From the rainbow sign to Jesus healing the sick and raising the dead, or Moses parting the Red Sea. We must take more notice of the miraculous and marvelous occurrences in our lives. We should especially be in awe over what God did for us when He sent Jesus to be the cornerstone of our salvation. Salvation is the most marvelous thing God has ever done in our lives. We will therefore rejoice and be glad.

Lord, your salvation is the most wonderful thing you have ever done in my life, and it is marvelous and miraculous in my eyes.

December 4
FLAWED BUT FAITHFUL

"Therefore we also, since we are surrounded by so great a cloud of witnesses,"

Hebrews 12:1a

My mother was the epitome of class and dignity. Look up the word "lady" in the dictionary, and there was a picture of my mom. I can still hear her in the back of my mind saying, "Should you wear a slip under that dress?" "Why don't you put on a little makeup?" And her favorite question throughout my college years when I would come home, "When is your next hair appointment?" The lady she was, my mom was flawed, she was a smoker. Even knowing the health risks associated with it, she continued to smoke until the time of her death. For a short time after she passed, I was hurt and angry and blamed her flaw for her death. God reminded me that we are all flawed sinners saved by grace. But God can still use us, flaws and all, to do his good works. Consider the faith hall of fame: Noah was a drunk (Genesis 9:21) but called a friend of God. Abraham was a liar (Genesis 12:13) but became the Father of Israel. Sarah was impatient (Genesis 16:2) but became the mother of the promised son. Moses was a murderer (Exodus 2:12) but became the deliverer. And Rahab was a fornicator (Joshua 2:1), but God called her faithful. God used all of them, flawed but faithful. What about us? No matter the flaw, if we give it to God, He can use us too.

Lord, use me, flaws and all for your faithful service.

December 5
I WON'T COMPLAIN

"And the people complained against Moses, saying, "What shall we drink?" So he cried out to the Lord, and the Lord showed him a tree. When he cast it into the waters, the waters were made sweet."

Exodus 15:24-25

My daughter is a picky eater, but she has a beautiful heart. Her face always betrays her words at dinner time. This happens whenever the menu doesn't contain something that she is fond of. Her mouth will say, "This is delicious" but her face says "This is gross." As Christians, we do a similar thing in our lives. Our mouths say, "Thank you, Lord" but our hearts say "No thank you." The good news is that God has promised us that even the bitter places of life will be made sweet if we trust God. We need not complain when life gets bitter. God specializes in bringing sweetness out of the bitter and hard places of life. When the children of Israel came to bitter waters, they complained instead of crying out to God. Moses, on the other hand, cried out to God. God then showed Moses what would make the bitter, sweet. Life is not always sweet. There is some bitterness in it. But as the songwriter said, "But when I look around, and I think things over, all of my good days, outweigh my bad days, I won't complain." Our response to the bitter places in life should be like Moses. We should cry out to God rather than complain.

Lord, instead of complaining let me always cry out to you in prayer when life gets bitter.

December 6
I'M DIFFERENT

"But My servant Caleb, because he has a different spirit in him and has followed Me fully, I will bring into the land where he went, and his descendants shall inherit it."

Numbers 14:24

I always loved Sesame Street as a child. I still enjoy watching with my children. One of my favorite segments was "One of these things is not like the others." The characters would sing, "One of these things is not like the others, One of these things just doesn't belong, Can you tell which thing is not like the others by the time we finish our song?" As Christians, we were not made to blend in but rather; we were made to stand out. People should see something different in the way we walk, the way we talk, and in our spirit. Note what God says of Caleb.

First, He calls him His servant. We serve God by reading His word to discover His will. We can then pray in His will and do those things He desires for us to do. Second, He said he had a different spirit. Caleb wasn't afraid to stand out in a crowd. He only wanted to serve the Lord. Finally, He said he followed God completely. Completely, without reservation or hesitation. The Bible reminds us continually of the blessings in obedience. We are different, and that is what God wants us to be.

Lord, let me stand out and not blend in so that others see a different spirit within me.

December 7
ALL OR NOTHING

"You shall love the Lord your God with all your heart, with all your soul, and with all your strength. "And these words which I command you today shall be in your heart."

Deuteronomy 6:5-6

I have a friend who is in a half-hearted relationship. They talk, sometimes but not often. The spend quality time together, occasionally. They almost never give gifts to one another, and when they do it is never an expensive gift, and there is no thought put into it. They aren't very honest in their communication with one another either. The relationship is covered in half-truths without honest communication. The worst part is that the relationship is not monogamous, my friend has some other love interests as well. Hopefully, this scenario doesn't sound familiar to you, but it may. It is a description of how many of us treat our relationship with the Lord. We don't talk to God often in prayer. We spend little if any quality time with Him. We don't give an offering regularly, let alone tithe. We don't even communicate honestly with God. Worst of all, we have put other people and interests before Him. Love is an action word. It is best expressed by doing. We are called to love God with all our heart ...with all our soul...with all our strength...He wants all our love or nothing at all. Most of all, He deserves it.

Lord, let me love you with my all, all my heart, all my soul, all my strength.

REQUIREMENTS NOT RESTRICTIONS

"And now, Israel, what does the Lord your God require of you, but to fear the Lord your God, to walk in all His ways and to love Him, to serve the Lord your God with all your heart and with all your soul, you today for your good?"

Deuteronomy 10:12

I am an environmental scientist for the government. Our world is full of requirements and restrictions. It is important that people understand the difference between the two. A requirement is defined as "something required, something wanted or needed, something essential to the existence or occurrence of something else." A restriction is defined as "a limitation on the use or enjoyment of property or a facility." Christians often struggle with aspects of the Word of God because we view it as restrictions or a list of "do nots." The reality is that God gives us restrictions so that we can successfully fulfill His purpose in our lives. God has requirements that identify us as His children. We are to walk with Him, love Him, worship Him, and keep His commandments. It is expected, not to restrict us but to equip us to walk in His will. God gives us requirements, but they are not restrictions.

Lord, let me stay focused on what you require of me and not being restricted.

December 9
BLESSINGS IN OBEDIENCE

"And all these blessings shall come upon you and overtake you, because you obey the voice of the Lord your God:"

Deuteronomy 28: 2

One of my favorite hymns of the church is "Trust and Obey." The lyrics of the first verse say, "When we walk with the Lord, In the light of His Word, What a glory He sheds on our way; While we do His good will, He abides with us still, and with all who will trust and obey." Then the chorus says, "Trust and obey, for there's no other way, to be happy in Jesus, but to trust and obey." We are blessed wherever we are. We are blessed in the city or the country. Others are blessed because of us. Our labor is blessed. We are blessed in our going and our coming. Our enemies are defeated. Our savings are blessed. We are blessed in everything we do. We will lend and not borrow. We are the head and not the tail. We will move up and not down. IF we follow the commandments of the Lord, there are blessings in obedience.

Lord, let me bless you with my obedience.

December 10

ALWAYS REJOICE

"Rejoice in the Lord always. I will say it again: Rejoice!"
Philippians 4:4 (NIV)

When I was a teenager, music remixes were very popular. An artist would release a song and then release a remix of the song. If a song was good, its remix would be even better. We would rejoice over the song remix! In life, we do not have to have a particular reason or season to rejoice. The Bible says that we are to rejoice always. In everything, we are to rejoice. Always rejoice.

Lord, let me rejoice in you and all of life's situations.

December 11
NOW UNTO HIM

"Now unto him that is able to do exceeding abundantly above all that we ask or think, according to the power that worketh in us,"
Ephesians 3:20

My favorite scripture is Ephesians 3:20. It has given me great hope in some of my most hopeless moments in life. The truth in its words came forth when my mother passed. People wondered why I wasn't completely falling apart. I explained to them that Ephesians 3:20 held me up, dried my tears, rocked me to sleep, and comforted me when I cried. I could find peace in knowing that God is able to do ANYTHING. "Now unto Him, the King eternal, immortal, invisible, the only wise God that is able to do exceedingly abundantly, above and beyond, all that we ask or think or believe or dream or imagine or pray or envision or wish.

Lord, let me always remember that you are able.

December 12
WHAT'S IN A NAME

"But now, God's Message, the God who made you in the first place, Jacob, the One who got you started, Israel: "Don't be afraid, I've redeemed you. I've called your name. You're mine."
Isaiah 43:1 (MSG)

After 38 years I decided to look up the meaning of my name. I had done it when naming both of my children but had never looked up the meanings of my first and middle name. I discovered my name, LaDonna Michele, means "Lady close to God." What joy there is knowing the significance of the meaning of your name! All my life I struggled with my testimony. I gave my life to the Lord when I was eight. I have often felt my testimony wasn't as strong as others because I never had a period of my life where I was far away from God. Now I understand, every time my parents said my name they were whispering a prayer for me to be close to God. Not only that, but God also called me by name. I am His. And so are you! God has called you by name; you are His. Our names have meaning in the light of God's love and grace.

Lord, thank you for calling us by name, giving our names meaning, and declaring us your own.

December 13
PRACTICE PRAYER

"Devote yourselves to prayer with an alert mind and a thankful heart."

Colossians 4:2 (NLT)

If at first you don't succeed, try, try, again." "Practice makes perfect." Successful people develop good habits and maintain daily discipline to keep those habits in place. Tom Bartow describes three phases of habit forming. The Honeymoon phase where we are driven by inspiration, The Fight Through phase where inspiration fades and reality sets in, and the Second Nature phase where we are getting into the groove. In the same way, if we want prayer to become a habit we must practice. The Bible tells us to devote ourselves to prayer with an alert mind and a thankful heart. An alert mind will let us know what to pray, and a thankful heart will lead us in how to pray.

Lord, help me be devoted to prayer with an alert mind and a thankful heart.

December 14
WE ARE FAMILY

"By the time David had finished reporting to Saul, Jonathan was deeply impressed with David—an immediate bond was forged between them. He became totally committed to David. From that point on he would be David's number-one advocate and friend."
1 Samuel 18:1 (MSG)

I don't have any siblings, but God has blessed me with an inner circle of sisters. These sisters are special because they are my framily—friends that I have chosen to make family. I can call, text, email, instant message, or GroupMe anytime. We have been through the good, the bad, and the ugly together. We are family. It reminds me of the friendship of Jonathan and David. It is a wonderful example of what a godly friendship is. The Bible says there was an immediate bond between them, they were totally committed to one another, and they were each other's number one advocate and friend. Godly friends are like family.

Lord, let me be and let me have godly friends who are totally committed and are each other's number one advocate and friend.

LaDonna Michele

December 15
PRAISE FOR PARENTS

"Listen with respect to the father who raised you, and when your mother grows old, don't neglect her. Buy truth—don't sell it for love or money; buy wisdom, buy education, buy insight. Parents rejoice when their children turn out well; wise children become proud parents. So make your father happy! Make your mother proud!"

Proverbs 23:22-25 (MSG)

I do not ever recall my daddy spanking me. My mommy yes, but my daddy, no (sorry dad). My dad was able to punish me with his words. Disappointing my dad to this day hurts me far worse than any spanking I ever received. Now that I am a parent, I want for my children the same things my parents wanted for me. I want my children to listen respectfully. I want them to get wisdom, education, and insight. I want to be able to rejoice at the academic and social maturation of my children. I want to be a proud parent. I want that not only for my children, but my godchildren, my friends' children, and all other children in my circle of influence.

Lord, let there be praise for all parents.

382

STOP THIEF

*"Will a man rob God? Yet you have robbed Me! But you say, 'In
what way have we robbed You?' In tithes and offerings."*

Malachi 3:8

The Chronicle of Philanthropy reported that donations
dropped at the nation's 400 biggest charities. Christians
give about 2.43 percent of their income, far less than the
biblical 10 percent tithe. With such statistics, it's almost like we
should expect to hear during offering time at church, "stop thief"
because we are robbing Him. We work diligently to give God our
best in almost every aspect of our Christian lives except one—our
finances. Few Christians give diligently of their treasure. If we give
God 10%, save 10%, and live off the 80%, God can do more with
80% than we can do with 100%. What's more, God has invited us
to try and see! We have nothing to lose!

**Lord, let me glorify you with my money because my money
has come from you.**

December 17
NO NEVER ALONE

"Let your conduct be without covetousness; be content with such things as you have. For He Himself has said, "I will never leave you nor forsake you."

Hebrews 13:5

I am an only child. When I was young, I hated being alone. I tried to keep a constant stream of friends spending the night at my house. It would work, sometimes. As I got older, I learned to appreciate being alone. Being by yourself does have some benefits. As Christians, we know that we are never really alone and there is great comfort in knowing that. One of my favorite hymns says, "No never alone. He's promised to keep me, never to leave me. No never alone." One of the blessed assurances that we have as children of God is that we are never alone. When trials come, we are not alone. When difficulties come, we are not alone. When death comes, we are not alone. When sickness comes, we are not alone. No never alone.

Lord, thank you for never leaving us alone.

December 18
NO TURNING BACK

"Do not remember the former things, Nor consider the things of old."

Isaiah 43:18

I asked my prayer friends what their lives were like before Jesus came into their lives. They said incomplete, lost, confused, gullible, vulnerable, selfish, broken, self-centered, empty, and prideful. Before we accept Christ, we are full of ourselves. After Christ, we are full of Him. We are full of Him if we choose not to look back. One of the hymns that accurately describes life with Christ is "I Have Decided to Follow Jesus." The lyrics say, "I have decided to follow Jesus;

I have decided to follow Jesus; No turning back, no turning back." Another verse says, "The world behind me, the cross before me...no turning back..." We cannot allow our past to hold us prisoner. We must keep pressing forward, no turning back.

Lord, let me stop allowing the past to hold me prisoner.

December 19
GRANDMA'S HANDS
AND MAMA'S WORDS

"I am reminded of your sincere faith, which first lived in your grandmother Lois and in your mother Eunice and, I am persuaded, now lives in you also."

2 Timothy 1:5 (NIV)

Bill Withers reminded us that "Grandma's clapped in church on Sunday morning. Grandma's hands, played the tambourine so well." According to The Shirelles, "mama said there would be days like this." The faith of our mothers and grandmothers is great, but we must cultivate a faith legacy of our own. Not only for ourselves but our children, grandchildren, nieces and nephews, cousins, and others. We can model faith and we can pass along our faith tradition. But at the end of the day, we must cultivate a faith walk for ourselves. We must come to the saving knowledge of Jesus Christ for ourselves. We can stand on the faith traditions of our mothers and grandmothers, but their faith will not save us. Thank God for grandma's hands and mama's words.

Lord, let me never forget the faith of my mother and grandmothers and give me a faith legacy to pass on myself.

December 20
NO SHAME IN MY NAME

"So do not be ashamed to testify about our Lord..."

2 Timothy 1:8a (AMP)

We underestimate the power of our testimony. We envy the testimonies of others. We keep our testimonies to ourselves. When in fact, we help others with the words of our testimony. We may be the instrument God chooses to break chains, loose shackles, and set others free. We need not be ashamed to tell others what God has done in our lives. Our testimony is when God became real in our lives, that's good news that needs to be shared. We find no shame in sharing half-truths, rumors, and gossip. We share without thought or reservation on Facebook. Let us be even more eager to share our testimony; someone needs to hear what we have to say.

Lord, thank you for saving me; may I never be ashamed of what you have done in my life and share my testimony with everyone I know.

December 21
STICK TO IT

"For the time will come when they will not endure sound doctrine, but according to their own desires, because they have itching ears, they will heap up for themselves teachers; and they will turn their ears away from the truth, and be turned aside to fables. But you be watchful in all things, endure afflictions, do the work of an evangelist, fulfill your ministry."

2 Timothy 4:3-5

Despite what you have heard, sin is a problem. A big problem. We begin the year with great spiritual ambitions. We plan to read our Bible daily, pray more frequently, grow in Christ, stop that sin. As the days proceed, we find ourselves fulfilling fewer and fewer of our spiritual goals. Why? Because of the sin we are in. In an age where information is so easily dispersed, we can easily become ensnared by strange doctrines. That is why it is more important than ever to know the truth for ourselves. We have to read and know for yourself. We have to stick to our convictions and spiritual goals.

Lord, sin is a problem, help sin not to reign in my life and me to keep my focus on you.

December 22
COUNT THE COST

"Suppose one of you wants to build a tower. Won't you first sit down and estimate the cost to see if you have enough money to complete it?"

Luke 14:28 (NIV)

Have you counted the cost for the last thing you asked God to do in your life? When we make requests of God, we sometimes negate to count what it will require of us. Do you want more money? Then you will be required to increase in stewardship. Would you like a promotion on your job? Then, you will be required to work harder. Would you like more patience? Then expect to be placed in more situation that will tempt you to be impatient. There is a cost for everything we desire from God. The question is, Are you willing to pay the cost?

Lord, help me to count the costs of everything you desire from me.

December 23
ALL IN HIM

"For in him all things were created: things in heaven and on earth, visible and invisible, whether thrones or powers or rulers or authorities; all things have been created through him and for him."

Colossians 1:16 (NIV)

I once heard a preacher say, "God took nothing and made something. Then God took something and made everything. God took nobody and made somebody. Then God took somebody and made everybody." All creation was spoken into existence by God. God is the creator and we are among the created. He created it all and us all. It is in Him all things were created, through Him, and for Him. It is all in Him.

Lord, all things were created in you, through you, and by Him.

December 24
DAILY RENEWAL

"Therefore we do not lose heart. Even though our outward man is perishing, yet the inward man is being renewed day by day."

2 Corinthians 4:16

Generations of explorers have sought the fountain of youth. The desire for physical renewal pushing them to the ends of the Earth. The truth is we were born to die. Job said, "Man is but a few days," and "Life is a vapor." But as believers, we are not discouraged. Though our physical bodies decline daily, our souls are renewed daily. Every day we are given new mercy, new chances. I am so glad that we serve a God not of a second chance but another chance. We used up our second and third chances a long time ago. Thank God for daily renewal.

Lord, thank you for renewal each day.

December 25
GIVE HIM GLORY

"And when they had come into the house, they saw the young Child with Mary His mother, and fell down and worshiped Him. And when they had opened their treasures, they presented gifts to Him: gold, frankincense, and myrrh."

Matthew 2:11

Christmas has become very commercial. There is Santa, Rudolph, The Grinch, and Elves on Shelves on center stage. If we are not careful, Christians will fix their focus on those things too. Giving our time and effort to commercialism when we should be giving glory to God. If we follow the example of the wise men, angels, and shepherds, that is exactly what we will do. The wise men brought Jesus gifts. What will you give Jesus? Your time, your talents, your treasure? The angels sang praises unto God. What songs fill your heart with joy? What hymns do you treasure in your heart? The shepherds bowed before Him and left glorifying God. At Christmas and all throughout the year, we ought to give God glory.

Lord, let everything I do give you glory at Christmastime and throughout the year.

December 26
BETTER NOT BITTER

"He heals the brokenhearted and binds up their wounds."
Psalm 147:3 (HCSB)

t is a fact that hurt people, hurt people. The question has even been asked, "What becomes of the broken hearted?" For many of us, the answer is we become bitter, depressed, angry, hateful and hurtful. However, we can rest assured that with Christ our broken hearts can be made whole. We can be confident that the wounds will heal. Christ turns our hurts into helps. He takes our hate and casts it out with love. Jesus takes our anger and makes us assist. He pulls us from depression into delight. God takes our bitter, broken hearts and makes us better.

Lord, thank you for making me better not bitter.

December 27
FIGHT AND HOLD ON

"Fight the good fight for the true faith. Hold tightly to the eternal life to which God has called you, which you have declared so well before many witnesses."

1 Timothy 6:12 (NLT)

Those things worth having in life are worth fighting for. That includes the natural as well as spiritual things. Not only that, the things of most value in life are worth holding on to. Family, friends, faith, morals, and on and on. All of these things are worth fighting for. The good fight of faith is day by day, sometimes hour by hour, or even moment by moment fight. The closer we strive to walk more closely with God and put on the character of Christ the more obstacles we will have to fight our way through. We need to hold on to our eternal life like it is our most prized possession because it is. Each day we need to fight and hold on.

Lord, empower me to day by day, hour by hour, even moment by moment, fight the good fight of faith and hold on to your precious gift of salvation.

December 28
THE MAIN THING

"One thing I have desired of the Lord, that will I seek: That I may dwell in the house of the Lord. All the days of my life, to behold the beauty of the Lord, and to inquire in His temple."

Psalm 27:4

We seek after a lot of things in life—love, career, clothes, status, money, fame, happiness. Although these are not necessarily a bad thing in and of themselves, they should not be the main thing in our lives. In pursuing these things, we should not lose sight of the main thing—God. The Psalmist said he only desired one thing, to dwell in the house of the Lord. His only desire was to be in the presence of God and talk to him. What is our primary desire? Is it to worship? Or to study God's word? Or to pray? Let's keep the main thing the main thing.

Lord, let my one desire be to dwell in your presence in all that I say and do.

December 29
FAIR WEATHER OR
THICK AND THIN FRIENDS

" Now when Job's three friends heard of all this adversity that had come upon him, each one came from his own place—Eliphaz the Temanite, Bildad the Shuhite, and Zophar the Naamathite. For they had made an appointment together to come and mourn with him, and to comfort him. And when they raised their eyes from afar, and did not recognize him, they lifted their voices and wept; and each one tore his robe and sprinkled dust on his head toward heaven. So they sat down with him on the ground seven days and seven nights, and no one spoke a word to him, for they saw that his grief was very great."

Job 2:11-13

There is one situation in life that will truly show you who your true friends are and that is death. In the face of death, real friends dig in and stick with you through the good, the bad, and the ugly. Death will reveal the fair-weather friends and the thick and thin friends. What is the difference? Thick and Thin friends come to you in the time of trouble, you don't have to call, and they come. Fair-weather may come if you call. Thick and Thin friends mourn with you, cry with you, grieve with you. Fair-weather friends might pass you a tissue or just a text. Thick and Thin friends may not know what to do to comfort you. But they hug you, console you, pray with you, pray for you, or just sit quietly with you not saying a word. Fair-weather friends don't know what to do, and so they do nothing. We should thank God for our thick and thin friends, our ride or die, and framily.

Lord, surround me with friends who will be with me through thick and thin and not just fair weather.

December 30

THE NEXT GENERATION

"Lord, You have been our dwelling place in all generations."

Psalm 90:1

I am blessed to be able to trace my family history back several generations on both my mother and father's sides. I know the names of both of my last slave ancestors. The fact that I am standing is a testament to the faith and endurance of the generations before me. Maya Angelou said it best when she wrote, "Bringing the gifts my ancestors gave; I am the hope and the dream of the slave." If it had not been for the Lord on the side of my ancestors, I don't believe I would be here today. The Lord has been the dwelling place of the previous generation. Not only that, God will be the dwelling place to the next generation if we keep the faith.

Lord, you have been, continue to be, and will remain our dwelling place.

December 31
MAKE A CHOICE

"And if it seems evil to you to serve the Lord, choose for yourselves this day whom you will serve, whether the gods which your fathers served that were on the other side of the River, or the gods of the Amorites, in whose land you dwell. But as for me and my house, we will serve the Lord."

Joshua 24:15

Life is full of choices. We wake up each day with choices to be made. Do I get up or press snooze? What will I wear? Do I eat breakfast at home or grab something on the way to work? Do I take the elevator or stairs? Cook or pick up dinner? Each choice has consequences, so we must choose wisely. The same is true with our daily spiritual walk. We must make spiritual choices each day. Will God be first today or self? Will I pray today or not? Will I read my bible? Do I help someone? The most important choice is, did I choose Christ and if I have, have I introduced anyone else to him? Each day we are faced with making a choice. Let us choose wisely.

Lord, let me choose daily to GROW in the character of Christ through prayer, study, and walking in your Word.

ABOUT THE AUTHOR

Author LaDonna Michele's name means a "lady close to God" and she considers herself a modern-day God-chaser. She has fallen in love with Jesus and strives daily to inspire others to fall in love with Jesus as well. Nicknamed "She-Barnabas," she works diligently to encourage others to grow in Christ.

LaDonna was born in Frankfurt, Germany, raised in Huntsville, Alabama and educated at the University of Alabama where she received both her bachelor's and master's degrees. She works full time as an environmental scientist for the US Army and part time as a geography instructor for a local community college.

She believes that every stumbling block is a stepping stone toward success. God is able. As her favorite scripture Ephesians 3:20 (MSG) states, "God can do anything, you know-far more than you could ever imagine or guess or request in your wildest dreams!"

She hopes this book inspires Christians of all genders, all ages, all experiences, and all levels of maturity to devote themselves to reading and praying daily to grow in God. That is why she wrote this devotional.

She is married to a God-fearing, loving husband and they have two children that look just like them. She and her family reside in Huntsville, Alabama. Read. Pray. GROW. is her first book.

ACKNOWLEDGEMENTS

Keen Vision Publishing
Studio 5 Design, Cover Design
Jenise Washington, Hairstylist (for author photo)
Colleen Gagnon, Makeup Artist (for author photo)
Joseph Merrell, Photography